Henry McAlpin

The messenger, a history of the class of 1881, of Princeton college

Henry McAlpin

The messenger, a history of the class of 1881, of Princeton college

ISBN/EAN: 9783337868079

Printed in Europe, USA, Canada, Australia, Japan

Cover: Foto ©ninafisch / pixelio.de

More available books at **www.hansebooks.com**

he Messenger.

1881.

BUDD,

Gentlemen's Outfitter

AND

SHIRT MAKER.

1101 Broadway, Madison Square,

NEW YORK.

The Messenger,

A HISTORY

OF THE

CLASS OF 1881,

OF

Princeton College,

BY

HENRY McALPIN, Jr.,

CLASS HISTORIAN.

———— ✦ ————

New York:
HORACE HOLDEN, Stationer and Printer, 6 Pine Street.

1881.

TO

The Members and Friends

OF THE CLASS OF '81,

THIS VOLUME IS DEDICATED,

WITH THE RESPECTS OF

THE AUTHOR.

Horace with sly insinuating glance,
Laughed at his friend and looked him in the face,
Would raise a blush when secret vice he found,
And tickled while he gently probed the wound.

—DRYDEN.

INTRODUCTION.

An author, by appearing in print, requesting an audience, should have something worthy of attention to offer or he will be justly deemed officious and impertinent. However, the thought of having my name placed on the title page of this book is so pleasing and flattering to my feelings, that I am contented to risk something for the gratification.

This preface is not designed to commend the volume to which it is prefixed, for the author fully appreciates its short-comings, but it is intended to call attention to the motives and intentions your author had, in writing some of the performances of his classmates.

It would be improper and unseemly for them to celebrate their own deeds. It has been our privilege to record events that may awaken a recollection of incidences and scenes which through the lapse of time they had almost forgotten. If in this volume any have been neglected or made too prominent, we ask the forgiveness of both.

To the first, we would say it was of course not intentional, for it has been our aim to record all incidences of interest that have occurred. We are fully aware, however, that many things have happened during our college course that never came to our notice.

To those made too prominent, we will say, it is not our fault they have made themselves notorious, but our duty as historian was to record such events as would lend interest to this history. We have at all times drawn things mild, and have endeavored to say nothing that would hurt the feelings or character of any one. In some instances we have deemed a hint sufficient to flood the mind of certain members of the class with recollections better appreciated through hints.

We fear that the form of this history will not be pleasing to the taste of all. We are aware that it is not strictly a historical form, but as all do not take interest in the same affairs, it seemed to us, that more general satisfaction would be given if like sports and incidences, could be found in their respective places under the several chapters.

It has been one of our chief aims in writing these articles to mention the members of the faculty as seldom as was possible without detriment to the history, but when any of them are spoken of in a seemingly light manner, the author had no intention of detracting in the least degree from their dignity.

Now your historian asks your leniency in criticisms; he is aware that much could be improved, but because it is not better is not because he has neglected his duty, but because he was unable to do more. May this volume, when the shadows of manhood are cast upon our now youthful faces, be to us a sacred grave yard, where many fond recollections are buried, but recall by the epitaphs many of the pleasant recollections crowded together in the four years of our college course.

CHAPTER I.

RUSHES.

On the 10th of September, 1877, the verdant spirits of '81 were seen flitting about the campus, most of them guarded by parents who sought this last opportunity to administer a parting warning, or give cheer to the now drooping spirits. They wandered from Museums to the Library, and from the " Gym " to Witherspoon.

Soon these parents leave us and we are launched upon our college course. The bell pealing out from North College warns us of the swiftly passing hours, and calls out to us that we are gradually leaving the shores of our boyhood and slowly, though scarcely perceptibly, approaching the haven of our manhood. Thus as the hours roll on we become more familiar with the objects that surround us, and more bold in assuming the duty of a *college man*.

Two days had passed since we had entered upon the arduous studies of Freshman year, and still we had heard nothing from those creatures, who had caused us so many *smiles* and blushes the previous June, and who were called " Sophs."

This quiescent attitude on the part of the Sophs. was not in accordance with the desires of the more pugilistic portion of our class, for they feared we would lose too much valuable time. They concluded to commence the attack, and accordingly a strip of paper was passed around the class, which read thus :

" There will be a gathering of '81 this evening in front of the Scientific School in order to rush the ' Sophs.' " Pass this on."

Many complied with this summons simply to satisfy their curiosity, for they wanted to see what kind of a thing a

" rush " was ; others'knew that it was some action against the " Sophs," and thought they were honor bound to help the class on to success.

Thus through many different motives the whole class was gathered together at the appointed time, and each one upon his arrival was crowded into the line that was then being formed, and were not allowed to leave even though their hearts failed them. It was a noble sight. There at the head of the class stood John Kirk, Vlymen, and Shaw, while at the other end could be *found* Dougall, Dodd, and Welles, with the rest of the class between them formed in rows of three each. This was the first time '81 had formed in a body to oppose anything. They certainly presented a formidable appearance ; determination was seen in every face, and we were ready to oppose any obstacle that might confront us.

We are formed ; all is ready for the conflict. Now in the distance is heard the strains of something singing to the class of '80. They are coming ; we stand in expectation ; the looked-for foe appears. The order " march " is given ; a shout ! a shock ! a pile of men ! The rush is over. After we regain our feet we hear much noise and quarrelling concerning the fairness of carrying a cane in a rush, but all ends with a victory claimed by both sides.

We are now aroused, we will rush anything—from a class of Sophs. to a stone fence, and, if necessary, will rush any number of times. Again we are formed into line, and set off with the determination to overcome and trample under foot any number of Sophs. it might be our fortune to meet. Our *line is* once more in motion, but this time we meet no host of Sophs., nor even a stone fence ; but some one yells the little word " Mat." There was something in the tone of his voice that indicated danger, and as the first few lines broke into disorder and scampered away across the campus, we all followed without inquiring the cause of this disorder. The little word " Mat " melted our line as the snow is melted beneath a spring day's sun. We run in every direction into the neighboring houses, and ARCHER, mistaking the house in which he lives, rushes through Mrs. ANDERSON's front door, up stairs into what he thinks his room, and hides himself in the closet. After his eyes have become accustomed to the darkness that surrounded him, and his mind ready to receive impressions, lo! much to his horror, he sees dresses, real female dresses, hanging in the place of his clothes ; he rubs his eyes and looks again, but still they are there. He cautiously opens the closet door and recognizes nothing about the room.

The idea that he is in the wrong house flashes across his mind ; in his imagination he can feel Mr. A. helping him out of the front door. He stealthily sneaks down the stairs, starting at the sound of every creaky step ; finally the door is reached, and the cool air of that fall evening fanning his heated brow restores him to quiet once more.

By this time the fellows have begun to leave their hiding places, and now gather around the object that caused our fright. This man " MAT " lets us know that we are to have no more rushing that night, consequently we retire to the streets, and there forming into line again march in triumph unmolested around the triangle singing

> Here's to '81, drink her down,
> Here's to '81, drink her down,
> Here's to '81, for she's always up to fun,
> Drink her down, drink her down, drink her down, down, down.

After marching round the cannon, and giving three cheers for '81, and three groans for '80, we went to our rooms and discussed in husky voices the fun of rushing. This was discussed with so much enthusiasm among a few that the next morning "ISTY," and one or two others, took the responsibility upon themselves to announce in a general way that there would be another rush that evening, but through some misunderstanding as to the time and place of our meeting, only a few of our fellows appeared. Those who on the night before came to the rush from curiosity, had been satisfied ; others also who did not relish the idea of having their heels trampled upon again,refrained from indulging a second time in this reckless sport. The few that did appear were formed into line at the foot of a hill, and here we awaited the "Sophs."

When our guardian Juniors who had so wisely formed us, found a defeat was inevitable, they ordered our lines to disband. All but the three first lines obeyed, and these nine men met the attack, but of course with no success.

SOPHOMORE RUSHES.

When we returned to college in September of Sophomore year, we determined not to let any of the Freshmen run over us as we had run over the Sophs. in our Fresh. year. We were prepared to meet them in anything they might propose, and showed before the year was past that we were more than a match for the combined energy of the Junior and Freshman classes ; the Juniors not only concocted the schemes for the Freshmen, but helped them to carry them into effect.

A few evenings, after the affairs of college were well started we agreed to rush the Freshmen on equal grounds, also that we would not molest them while they were forming, but when they were ready to rush they could come within a certain distance of us before they could be rushed. After the settlement of all these preliminaries they formed down Bayard Avenue and we by the Episcopal Church.

The Freshmen numbered many more than we did, and our line was extra short because those of our class who had been suspended the year before did not dare enter upon the violation of the college laws so soon after recrossing the threshold of their college course. With Kirk, Vlymen and Shaw again in the front line, and ten encouraging voices from the pavement, we looked very formidable to the Freshmen.

The Freshmen indulged in a lengthy preparation, but their advance was announced by a herald. We waited until they crossed the mark agreed upon ; here they seemed to falter, and we, seizing the opportunity rushed down upon them, putting their line into confusion. We mashed a few of them against an iron fence until they begged for quarter. We granted it, and they scampered away as fast as they could go and did not appear again upon the scene of action.

All the Freshmen that remained, formed again into line, and at a short distance, we stood facing them. Both lines moved towards each other, then came the shock—their line bends, and they rush each other, and we again, without any difficulty push our way through them, and another victory is scored for us. We might have continued this sport until the Freshmen grew sick of defeat, had not " MAT " put in an appearance, which was sufficient to stop the rushing. We marched around the town singing—

" I wish I had a little Freshman."

A little later in the year the Freshmen showed some signs of precociousness, so a few of our class concluded it would do the Freshmen good to take them down a little, and not allow them to get their mamma's letters that evening.

SELHEIMER, MONROE, and some others, appeared at the Post-office earlier than usual, and arranged themselves so that when a Freshman appeared inclined to get his mail they could send him out of the door faster than he had entered, or else close around him in a way more affectionate than agreeable to him. After a few had been shot from the door, there appeared one upon the scene of action, more bold than the others, who attempted to come in, but GREER MONROE considered it his duty to make him go the way the other Freshmen had gone, and accordingly the verdant youth suddenly disappeared, only to return enraged. He dared GREER to come out, and before the Freshman knew what he was doing, he found himself knocked over in the mud. DENNIS came to see GREER the next day, and GREER left town for a week on business.

The Freshmen were forming in the street to come into the office in a body, but before they knew what we intended doing next, we rushed upon them in a body, and they ran in all directions ; then we returned to the office. By this time the Postmaster had become infuriated, and was "spotting" all the fellows that he knew, we concluded that it was about time for us to leave, and marched out into the street again, but " DINKS " was violently pulled from the line and seated in the muddy ditch. " I will thrash the man that did that," said DINKS, but changed his mind when he saw that it was the handiwork of our dwarfish Proctor.

Don't shorten this
Index. The loan is
for TWO WEEKS.

FEB 13

CHAPTER II.

OUR LIBRARIAN.

One day shortly after our entering college WELLES wentinto that beautiful structure the Library. It was his first visit to that building. He walked in with wondering gaze, in one hand he held his hat, and in the other a book which he had just been using in the recitation room. Scarcely had he entered the door and begun to feast his eyes on the beauties around him, when he saw a little grim-looking man descend from what seemed to him a sentinel box. He had not time to collect his thoughts; he felt a tug at his arm, and heard a nasal voice say "Read this." When WELLES sufficiently recovered himself he saw confronting him a framed document which was headed "Laws of the Library." In casting his eyes hurriedly over the first rule he found that it required him to leave his hat and book in the hall before entering the room. Obeying this order, WELLES quietly retired to the Hall and deposited his hat and book, but the look of the little man had made an indelible impression upon his youthful mind, and it was with timidity that he re-entered the room. In admiring the building he only used one eye, for the other was kept busy in watching the movements of his friend whom he saw was scrutinizing him with a withering glance.

The idea flashed across WELLES that he wanted a certain book, but he did not altogether like the idea of asking any assistance from the gentleman behind the railing, so he continued his efforts but in vain, and finding he was not likely to discover the volume he wished, he cautiously approached the cage-like stand.

When about to ask for the desired information Mr. V. shot the following interrogation at him:

Mr. V.—Well, what do you want?

WELLES.—Where, sir, can I find *Miss Mühlbach's* Queen Hortense?

Mr. V. (*In a loud tone of voice*)—First, would you expect to find it among the Scientific works, or is it Historical?

WELLES.—(*Frightened almost to death*)—Among the Historical, sir.

Mr. V.—If it is Historical, would you expect to find it among the Modern or Ancient works?

WELLES.—Among the Modern, I should think, sir.

Mr. V.—If it is among the Modern Historical works, then would you look for it in the prose or poetical alcove?

WELLES (*Looking for a way out of the Library*)—I don't know, sir.

Mr. V.—Now, think! what kind of a book is it?

WELLES.—It is a novel.

Mr. V.—What kind of a novel?

WELLES.—Historical.

Mr. V —Well, then, would you look in the fiction or historical alcove?

WELLES.—In the fiction alcove, sir.

Mr. V.—Certainly! Why do you not look there then?

Here WELLES was discouraged, for he knew in the first instance that the book must be in the fiction alcove, but that was what he could not find.

When he made this known to Mr. V., that worthy gentleman called his attention to a sort of schedule on the desk, and told WELLES he could find out from that.

After many vain attempts to decipher this schedule, he came to the conclusion that it was intended to show where the books ought to be, but from it he could learn nothing. He made known to Mr. V. his inability to read this scroll. At this announcement Mr. V.'s eyes flashed fire, his lips grew ashy and quivered with anger; he burst forth in a most enraged tone, and accused WELLES of attempting, under the mantle of ignorance, to annoy him, and said that if he heard anything more from him he would summon MAT GOLDY and have him ejected from the building. At this juncture WELLES almost swooned away. First, at being so falsely accused, and secondly, at the idea of having "MAT" come after him.

He mustered up energy enough to dive for the door, and had almost laid his hand upon the knob, when he was again startled by the familiar voice calling after him, "Come back here! where are you going?"

Another mistake had been made by him. He had almost entered the Trustees' room instead of the Hall in which he had left his hat.

After receiving another lecture upon his impudence, impertinence, and precociousness, he was put upon the right path, and waiting only long enough in the Hall to seize his hat, he shot from the door leaving his book behind him. If we are to believe rumors, WELLES never crossed the threshold of that building again during Freshman year.

CHAPTER III.

BOATING.

The boating interest in College was at its lowest ebb when the class of '81 entered among the number entitled to the use of the boat-house, and a place on the " Raging Raritan canal."

Our class was unusually blessed with lovers of this aquatic sport, so numerous in fact were the applicants for a place on the class crew that it was determined to allow GEORGE GOLDY to pick out twelve men whom he thought best built for oarsmen.

On the appointed day about thirty candidates presented themselves at the " Gym.," and held themselves in readiness for the inspection ; among this number were seen CRAVEN, KIRK, BOCOT, " FATTY " RYLE, LANG, MIKE O'RYAN, and others.

After much thumping, expanding, and hardening of muscles, it was announced that twelve men had passed their physical examination, and that, that afternoon they were to be subjected to their o(a)ral examination on the canal.

That afternoon the twelve men presented themselves at the canal. The rowing was done under the supervision of Mr. JOHN McGAW W. He ran along the bank by the side of our boat and wildly gesticulated to us, calling out first to starboard and then to port, to pull harder, to keep their backs straight, etc. He called to each of these sides so often that BILLY COURSEN's curiosity was aroused, and he asked the man next to him who was named *Starboard* and *Port* in the boat. This remark was appreciated by all in the boat, and BILLY's ignorance of nautical terms ruined his chance for the crew. Our actions so enraged our coach that he swore by

Neptune and all his train, that if we did not keep our eyes
in the boat we would never learn to row.

Out of the two crews that were fairly tried that afternoon
only seven were considered capable of training up in form
during the short time allotted to us before the race.

Within a few days the number had dwindled down to
BILLY ROBERTS, TOMMY BRADFORD, McDERMONT, WEST. LYND,
and another. These five rowed diligently every day, while
the sixth seat was always filled by a new man.

The time passed on and still the crew was not chosen.
Our *coach* always found some fault with the new victim, and
discarded him only to choose another.

Those of our class who watched our movements with
growing anxiety and interest became impatient for the choosing of the sixth man, and urged the necessity upon the five
already chosen to assume command and settle this point
themselves. This they soon did, and the following crew was
to represent us in the class races : BILLY ROBERTS, stroke
and captain ; McDERMONT, No. 5 ; BRADFORD, No. 4 ;
McALPIN, No. 3 ; WARREN, No. 2 ; and WEST LYND pulled
bow. In this crew rested our hopes for great deeds, for
things never before done in the annals of college boating, and
conceived only in the youthful mind of the dreaming enthu-
siast.

Our crew made such wonderful progress in their rowing
that the other two crews who at first feared little from us
now grew anxious as to the result of the coming race. The
time appointed for the race soon drew near, and the day
soon came on which we shipped our shell for Burlington,
which had been chosen as the scene of the contest.

At noon, on the 12th of October our crew, with their boat,
were nicely settled on the Delaware, and were the guests of
the " Oneida Boat Club," of Burlington.

We had hoped to have been able to have rowed over the
course that morning, but the Delaware appeared to us more
formidable than the raging Raritan had done.

We sat mournfully upon the float of the boat-house watching the huge waves lash themselves to foam upon the rockbound shore, and we often, with a sigh, wished that the wind would die away, and allow us to ply our oars upon the placid bosom of this now boisterous stream.

That afternoon, much to our delight, our wish was fulfilled, for the waves so greatly subsided that we ventured upon the river in our light craft. After a few short moments of anxiety we became more at home upon this stream, and glided easily down the river. So evenly did we pull that the other two crews feared us more than ever, and our motions were highly commended by the spectators who watched us from the boat-house.

After tea, guided by an inhabitant of the town, the three crews visited, by the light of the moon, a grand building which was used as a young ladies' seminary. We had no intention of making any disturbance in the school; oh, no! but only wanted to catch a glimpse of some of the smiling countenances, and thought the sweet strains of music might bring about the desired end. In order that we might the more plainly be heard, and could the better see without being seen, we entered the grounds and hid ourselves in the deep shadows cast by the towers of the building. The note was struck, and with one accord, but many a discord, the tune was raised and swelled with eighteen voices. All hopes of order in the school room was lost, the girls rushed to the windows, threw them open, and showed their hearty approval of our musical talent. We now became enthusiastic and cheered them vociferously, when suddenly BILLY ROBERTS felt a firm grasp upon his muscular arm, and looking round, he found a man very diminutive in stature held him. He reprimanded BILLY in the most furious tones for daring to come into his enclosure. BILLY blandly smiled, and the man, who proved to be the principal of the school, growing more furious, informed " BILLY " that he was the one in whose care three hundred young ladies were intrusted, and that he did not intend to be smiled at in that sarcastic manner. BILLY suggested to the old gentleman that he must be a very happy man.

The rest of the party had by that time retired to the gate, and still BILLY lingered ; he seemed to have no idea of leaving so soon, such a field for mashers. Things were changed ! The little man finding his commanding manner did little in over-awing BILLY, called his bull " purp," and BILLY immediately sought refuge on the nearest fence, but left a mouthful of the leg of his pants with the female protector. It is said that a young lady the next morning found this piece of gentleman's wearing apparel and has kept it as a memento ever since.

When success seemed ours and each one's hopes were raised to their highest pitch, blind fortune in an unlucky hour dashed the cup of bliss from our lips.

The night previous to the day of the race, HARRY WARREN was taken sick, and we found that he would not be able to row. We had no substitute, and could not think of anything that could be done. In our despair it seemed as though we would be unable to row, and as a last resort we accepted the services of one who had been very kind to us in supervising our training but who was not himself trained, and he it was who filled the vacant seat.

The hour for the race at last came. The merry throng of fellows wandered to the banks of the river. Here were gathered together all of the inhabitants and beauties of Burlington. It was an inspiriting sight. Our crew, cheered by the yells of encouragement sent up by our classmates, rowed slowly down to the starting point.

All were in position, the time drew near for the word " Go !" Three crews bent forward on oars waiting in breathless expectation for this word. It came, and like three arrows shot from the same bow they started off together.

We held our place until we reached the end of the first mile, when the new man gave out and became a dead weight.

From that time we lost ground but came in a very good third. After the excitement of the race was over the fellows sought the depot and then with song and laughter we waited for the arrival of the train which was to bear us to our destination. As the engine came thundering up the track "General" MYERS, who was a little *elated* from some unknown cause wanted to buck the locomotive off the track, but was prevented before any harm was done to the train.

By eight o'clock that evening Burlington was cleared of all Princeton students, and once more the old-fashioned place settled into its wonted tranquility and peace.

On our way home that evening POWERS FARR was holding the cane of a portly Junior, when a Sophomore came up to him, and in a very unceremonious manner demanded the stick. POWERS refused to give up the cane intrusted to his keeping; at this refusal the Sophomore seized the cane, and a struggle ensued; they were evenly matched, and tumbled around the car promiscuously, knocking off the hats and "specks" of old gentlemen and, it is said, then caught in the bonnet strings of an old lady, which took off her head gear, and *snatched her bald-headed*.

The tussel went on for some time, but at last POWERS threw the "Soph." into a plate glass door of the car making a wreck of it. At this critical moment the conductor came in and demanded the stick, at which request POWERS yielded his hold and the "Soph" took the cane from the conductor's hands, who became so enraged that he made the Sophomore pay for the glass. At that time the Junior came in and demanded his property, which was yielded up without any controversy. It proved a dear fight for the Sophomore and a feather in POWER'S cap, because his antagonist was one of the strongest men in '80.

CHAPTER IV.

RECEPTIONS.

Never wedding, ever wooing,
Still a love lorn heart pursuing,
Read you not the wrong you're doing,
In my cheeks pale hue ?
All my life with sorrow strewing
Wed, or cease to woo.
—CAMPBELL.

Shortly after our return from the Christmas vacation in Freshman year our class received invitations to a reception given by one of the Professors at his house in our *honor*.

We were greatly elated and excited about it and whenever any of the fellows passed each other they would make some remark about " going to the ball."

Much to our delight the evening at last came and we waited in joyful expectation for the arrival of the hour at which we were to make our entrance into Princeton society. SYMMES misconstrued his invitation, as it read " tea from six until ten." He concluded he would not keep the family waiting for him, and he also thought he would get the first pick at the things to eat, so he went at five. The Professor and his family were just sitting down to a light repast when SYMMES was ushered into the parlor. He was invited to come in and have a little tea, which invitation he of course accepted. After they had finished, he thought he was expected to arrange the table for the next comers, so, much against the wishes of the host, he helped to arrange the supper table. He was at last disturbed from his occupation by hearing that some young ladies had arrived. He thought that part of his duty as a favored guest was to help entertain them, so he left the dining room for the parlor. Here he made himself very agreeable, until HUDNUT was ushered in. SYMMES rushed up to him, shook his hand, in one breath he welcomed him, and asked him if he had had anything to eat. There is no telling what he would have done, had not the fellows at this time arrived too fast for him to attend to.

The young ladies of the town were the only ones that had been fortunate enough to be invited to this Freshman reception; they, however, were all new to us, but unfortunately were few in number, consequently the male persuasion were in the majority, and those fellows who were able to get near enough to a young lady to be introduced considered themselves lucky.

It was an animated sight! Princeton's fairest daughters surrounded by a host of admirers who stood with open mouths, all anxious to say something which they could not, because of the incessant conversation kept up by the ladies. In other parts of the room were gathered groups of fellows discussing the subject of dancing, and how soon it would begin; how long before supper would be ready, and sometime athletics became the topic of conversation. Some few unfortunate fellows who were not lucky enough to be among the chosen satellites, and who could not become interested in the conversation of the fellows, because they were painfully aware that there was to be no light fantastic tripped that evening, were seen wandering listlessly about the room looking at pictures or books, or doing anything that would consume the time until supper should be announced.

When at last we were invited to partake of the repast prepared for us, those fellows who had previously secured partners, marched triumphantly into the supper room. To some of the fellows who had to escort themselves, I am indebted for the following incidences of the occasion :

" DINKS " had been Miss R'—'s escort. After a slight pause in the conversation which they had kept up, Miss

R. said, Mr. Landon, how do you like 'Spencer's Fairy Queen?'" What in the world was Spencer's Fairy Queen? thought Dinks; Was it something to eat? for they had just been talking of fancy dishes. These were his thoughts when Miss R. saw the puzzled expression upon his face and asked him "Which of Spencer's works he liked best?" Then it flashed across his mind that it must be an author, and he thought "he liked that one she had just mentioned," but, said he, "I have never read many of her works." Carlyle was next mentioned, and met with about the same result. In a short time after these themes had been discussed, "Dinks" escorted Miss R. into the parlor and soon after excusing himself he inquired of Stuart Brown about Carlyle, Stuart thought for a moment and then said that he did not know where Carlyle was, but he thought Carl-Helaum was on Nassau street.

Billy Roberts stood with a plate of ice cream in his hand and smiled at Miss A., who smiled again at him. Billy said something, and took three or four large teaspoons full of cream in quick succession, and Miss A. quietly said " Yes." Then came a pause, during which Billy saw a figure flit by him. Like a sunbeam breaking through a cloudy sky came a thought to Billy which illuminated his whole countenance. He gathered together all his reserved energy and said "I feel so sorry for poor old Stevy, his legs are so little and they—." There is no telling what he would not have said, for he had a good start, but he was stopped in his mad career by Miss A., who interrupted him with the remark, "He is my father." Billy blushed to the roots of his hair when he thought what he had said, and to make it worse it was about the parent of his partner. Another silence followed, his thoughts made this the most painful silence he had ever experienced. At this break in the conversation the host came up and asked them to have some more *soup*, this they both simultaneously declined, and soon betook themselves to the parlor. Shortly after they had become settled upon the sofa, and had resumed their usual animated conversation, GUS WEBB was brought up and presented to Miss A. BILLY excused himself, and GUS opened the conversation with Miss A. by asking her if this was her first visit to Princeton? She blandly smiled, and said she had lived in Princeton all her life. GUS then started on the weather for he thought it time to change the topic.

There was now but one couple left in the dining room. The reason for their staying so long was not because of the amount they had eaten, but because "SOONER" FOWLER who was not a large eater, was such a terrible talker; even in "Fresh." year he was very entertaining because of the large supply of funny stories he knew. It was on account of the numerous anecdotes that he had told Miss M. during the repast, that made them linger so long around the festive board. He was talking in his dry manner when some fellow happened to hear him say something about an old graduate returning to his *alma mater*, and in connection with the graduate and his room, "SOONER" in some way brought in the remark about the *same old game*.

The young lady was seen to smile and slightly blush. SOONER cleared his throat and made another remark, at which Miss M. said: "I am afraid you are an artful *fowler* and you are giving me taffy, but I am too old a bird to be caught by such chaff." At this instant PENN WHITEHEAD was introduced to Miss M., and SOONER left. By this time the fellows had greatly thinned out, and it was on account of this that PENN was able to monopolise the attention of Miss M. He had just fairly started upon his usual rapid manner of talking, when he was interrupted by hearing a small still voice say: "Come, daughter, fold up your tent like the wandering Arab and silently steal away."

PENN thought it was about time for him to leave.

𝕾𝖔𝖕𝖍𝖔𝖒𝖔𝖗𝖊 𝕽𝖊𝖈𝖊𝖕𝖙𝖎𝖔𝖓,

UNIVERSITY HOTEL,

Monday Evening, June 16th, 1879.

AT TEN O'CLOCK.

ADMIT GENTLEMAN AND TWO LADIES.

This feature of commencement, which in '79s Soph. year had proved a brilliant success not only in enjoyment but as a means for making the classic shades of Princeton more brilliant with female beauty, seemed to all the lovers of the mazy dance just the thing wanted to add some life to the week devoted to speechmaking. After due consideration, a committee of thirteen was elected by the class, whose duty it was to make all necessary arrangements and make the evening as enjoyable as possible.

This committee was composed of BLYDENBURGH, BRUCE, FARR, HARLAND, INGHAM, LANDON, LONEY, McALPIN, MUNN, PITNEY, A. SCRIBNER, VANDYKE and WEBB.

Soon after their election, they had a meeting, discussd the best way to work, and the many things necessary to do. The work was divided into different parts and a committee for each part was appointed. Many were the meetings held by them, and long the discussions as to the most economical and successful manner of transacting the business.

After much worry and anxiety, mingled with the pleasure of anticipation, the evening came. We drew a sigh of relief to think it had come so near to being a realization, but eight o'clock was sounded from the chapel clock and no musicians had made their appearance. The committee grew anxious; silent thoughtfulness was seen in the face of every member of the committee. What could be done, should not the music come? This and many other such remarks escaped their lips from time to time, but when at last, hope had almost died out, the music came and the ball was set in motion.

Seldom indeed has Princeton witnessed so brilliant a scene. The walls of the rooms had been decorated with perfect taste. Suits of mail reflected from their polished surfaces the rays of the brightly-lighted hall, and made it still more brilliant; flags of all nations were draped upon the walls; the orange and black hung in graceful festoons from the ceiling. Such an array of female beauty was never before gathered in one hall. "Eyes looked love to eyes which spake again, and all went merry as a marriage bell."

Here Beauty to Art was wed, without sacrificing any of its simplicity in the alliance. The porches, curtained in and dimly lighted, afforded many recesses where those weary of dancing might find rest.

The sweetness of soft music was wafted hither on the summer breath. With these surroundings, those who had never before now felt the sensation, became *romantic*. Even CHARLEY MUNN was heard to indulge in the following conversation:

CHARLEY (*looking pathetically into Miss M.'s face*)—"Miss M., I feel that now I am nearer heaven than ever before. Those eyes, like stars, sparkle best at night. That expression, most divine, makes you a goddess at whose altar I am an earnest devotee, and I worship the ground you walk upon."

MISS M.—"Oh! Mr. MUNN, how you flatter, and I do not like flattery."

CHARLEY.—"I do not flatter, but speak the truth, which comes from no other source than my heart. I repeat it, I love you, and——"

Miss M.—"But Mr. Munn, you have not known me half an hour."

Charley.—"That matters not; I loved you even before I knew you. I was bewitched by those bright eyes, that silvery musical voice, and—ah—do you love me?"

Miss M.—You did not attract my attention before I met you, and you must remember you are only a *sophomore*."

Charley was about to make some remark when Gus. Webb came up and claimed Miss M. for the next dance, and Munn was left alone in silent meditation.

Many such incidents made the evening memorable.

Nothing happened to mar the pleasure connected with such an entertainment, and although the room was crowded, the evening passed rapidly and pleasantly. Many of our class, who had not dress suits of their own, borrowed them. "Isty" wore Dave Haynes' coat, and made many "mashes."

When the festival was over, and the sounds of dancing had ceased, the moon had just set in the west; the morning star had begun to fade; the calm glories of the night were beginning to lift from all around. The first blush of morning was seen in the eastern sky and chanticleer ushered in the coming day when we reluctantly left the hall, not without feeling that lassitude which always follows earthly joy, no matter how sweet.

CHAPTER V.

CANE SPREES.

The eighteenth of September, 1877, was a memorable day for our class. All during the morning we were greatly excited, for that evening the preliminary cane spree was to take place. Who was to represent our class we knew not. The choosing of the proper one we had left to our guardian Juniors.

At about eight o'clock that evening, the crowd, which had been for some time accumulating about "East," form·d themselves into a ring, in the midst of which stood two dumpy-looking men, whom we soon found out to be the contestants. Four men at first held the cane, but at a certain signal two took their hands off; the other two, who were stooping over the cane, with their heads in close proximity, proved to be the champions, who held the reputation of the class at stake. From the twisting and turning that followed we saw the fight had begun. We heard the "Sophs" cheering on their man and calling him pet names. We were unacquainted with the nomenclature of our representative and simply yelled, " Go in '81, that was a good one!" " Give him another, '81 !" &c. Eighty-one did go in, and gave him several more, but without success, nor could the "Soph" gain anything from his tricks and one year's experience. They were so evenly matched that neither could take the cane. After a long but plucky fight, it was determined to cut this *fated wand*. This we considered a victory for us. It rested with the Sophomore to take the cane from our man, but as he was unable to do so we claimed that our man was champion. He was raised on our shoulders, and we started off on a triumphant march. We rent the air with wild discord in singing praises to JOHN KIRK.

A few nights after the preliminary cane spree, each member of our class having previously secured a guardian Junior and a cane, met at the north end of "Dickerson" and marched to the grass plot back of "East." Upon our arrival there was so much yelling that we could scarcely hear ourselves think.

The matches which had been previously arranged were soon started. LONEY took a cane in about two seconds, which greatly surprised the Sophomore. BRADISH was fortunate enough to get a small man, and shook his head almost off of him.

At different points of the field the Seniors could be seen feeling the muscular development of Freshmen before intrusting their wards into the Freshmen's clutches. The Junior who had charge of BILLY BACOT told him not to harden his muscles when a Senior wanted to see how strong he was, but to let his arm appear as soft as possible BILLY, indignant at this advice, drew himself up to his Freshman height and said : "Would you have me deceive them? Oh no, Sir, I will not enter upon this contest if I will have to do anything of that kind." His Junior told him that he could do as he chose. BILLY frightened away several "snaps;" finally a man took him, and, after a short struggle, BILLY yielded up the cane.

The cheers given, announcing a victory for each side, at first were faint, but as the evening passed away and the fights became fewer in number, the crowds became concentrated and the yells more intense. When, in the middle of the evening, McDERMONT took a cane from one of the "brag" men of the Sophomore class, the fellows rushed frantically about, hugging each other and exhibiting most peculiar demonstrations of delight.

The fights ultimately dwindled down to one, and this was represented by BRUCE. He had begun among the first in the evening, and had hung on until he was now the last. The judges had agreed to cut the cane at a certain time if neither had taken it. The time drew near; ten seconds were called. BRUCE made one more desperate effort and took the cane before time was called. This, of course, produced wild excitement, and "East College" shook with the cheers that went up on this occasion.

The next morning the class was canvassed, and it was found by actual count that we took seven more canes than the Sophomores.

SOPHOMORE YEAR.

The evening agreed upon proved to be mild and clear ; the fellows gathered on the front campus to witness the test of strength. The ring was in due time formed, and we were ready to match any man '82 saw fit to bring out. In the middle of the circle stood a large man muffled to his ears, who challenged any man in our class. KIRK was called upon, and once more our champion of Freshman year entered the arena, this time to gain a more decided and brilliant victory than he had gained the year before.

After the usual amount of discussing and arguing was ended, and all of the necessary preludes completed, the fight began. The Freshman seemed to be a larger man than JOHN. The fight at first looked doubtful, but through a dextrous twist and turn on the part of JOHN we scored a victory. Our champion was once more lifted to our shoulders, while the Freshman giant was allowed to find consolation in solitude.

After the usual amount of noise that generally follows such a coincidence, the fellows quietly settled down. A second ring was formed, and a second victim led in.

In this man the Freshmen were certain of success. He had been training under a professional coach all Summer, and for that reason they had great confidence in his abilities.

LONEY was chosen from our class as a match for him. Scarcely had the judges released their holds of the cane when the Freshman was sprawling upon the ground, having released his hold of the cane as he passed over LONEY's hips. This was another ignominious defeat for the Freshmen and a victory for us.

GENERAL CANE SPREE.

The general contest came off much later this year than it did the year before. A moon light night was what the Freshmen were waiting for, because they wanted to see what they were doing.

On the evening appointed for the spree, BRANT, BEDELL and a few others laid in wait around the Campus for any Freshman who might be taking a cane to his room to use that evening. After some time had elapsed without their having captured any prizes, they saw a Freshman who looked rather sheepish and walked without much bend in one knee. BRANT accosted him, saying, " Freshman, you have a cane in your breeches leg, and you must give it to me." The Freshman meekly unbuttoned his vest and drew out a nice stick, during which action he apologized for having it about him, but he did not want to make his Junior go after it. BRANT took the cane, and told the Freshman that it was against the rules for them to carry even concealed canes. BEDELL accosted another Freshman in the same manner, who yielded after a little resistance. No more canes were confiscated by them, for those two Freshmen warned the others, and none of them passed that way.

The hour of the spree at length arrived, and the Freshmen marched to the field of " *Cane-on*," back of Reunion.

Among the noticeable fights of the evening were those of DAVE RICKETTS, who did good work. BRADFORD, after a hard fight, took a cane from another of '82 brag men. BILLY BACOT reformed this year and *did* NOT harden his muscles; the consequence was he took a cane. POWERS FARR made an interesting and successful fight. Some of our best men, however, were unable to get any one to take them. One of them was so anxious to fight that he offered to take a man his own size, on the conditions that if he did not take the cane in five minutes he would give it up. Even this could not induce the Freshman to take him.

The result of the evening's sport was an overwhelming victory for us.

CHAPTER VI.

MISCHIEF.

What boy did mortal ever find,
Who bred no mischief in his mind?

There is a time in every Freshman year at which a certain
crowd in the class become perfectly familiar with their new
surroundings, and grow easy in the every-day course of college life. At this period the chosen few are generally over-
taken by the desire to pass beyond their usual work and enter
into the realms of Mischief, whose deeds are mantled by the
dark shades of night. The desire to do aught that approaches
harm is not for a moment sustained by them, but the height
of their ambition is to get ahead of any one who attempts to
thwart them in the accomplishment of their plans. If they
are frustrated in an attempt to obtain a desired object, they
become more eager to procure it. Taking things owned by
others (who are known to be on their guard) is not considered
stealing, but is looked upon as a good joke.

Stimulated by these principles and desires, in an innocent
way we accomplished much mischief. It became our ambition to excel in deeds of mischief all other Freshman classes,
and to leave behind us a record which would be difficult to
beat. Many evenings were consumed in concocting schemes
and putting into effect deeds which would worry "Mat,"
and also make our names memorable. In the execution of
these plans we succeeded wonderfully well. The town still
lacks some of its gilt-edged ornaments, and occasionally we
hear the vibration of some of our Freshman year deeds.

Among the first worthy of notice was that of the duck hunt,
which was brought about as follows : One evening a party of
nine, consisting of TOMMY BRADFORD, "JOHN BULL," BRADLEY,

"Dinks," Loney, McDermont, "General," Harry Payne, and
another, met together in Landon's room to discuss projects
of mischief and deeds that would make the history interesting. After the proposal and rejection of many plans, it was
ultimately settled that we would make an attempt to obtain
the fly-wheel of the organ, and prevent, for some little time,
any music from that instrument. We however knew that the
attempt would be impracticable until the early hours of the
morning, for some of us had previously happened by accident
to be out a little after the bell had rung for us to be in our
rooms, and had found the Campus well guarded. We concluded that it would be better for us to wait until the hours
of the night " when sleep comes over the faithful watchman."
"What is to be done until that time?" asked Dinks ; for he
felt then a little sleepy, and did not like to pass into the stage
of peaceful oblivion with so many visitors around. "General" Myers, with his usual quickness, came to our assistance and suggested duck-hunting. We all agreed to do anything he told us, and appointed him guide. The "General"
then explained to us, in his own peculiar way, how not far
away in a quiet little pond could be found *lots of ducks*. After
he had entered into minute details as to the location of the
pond, he suggested that we should approach this point in
companies of twos or threes, and at a certain time concen-
trate our forces at Jugtown, assuring us that " we would have
more fun than a barrel of monkeys."

We armed ourselves with a pillow-case drawn from
"Dinks'" bed, which we intended to use as a game-bag.

At the appointed hour these several divisions entered the
city of Jugtown from different directions. Here "General"
Myers held a consultation of war, and gave his opinion as to
the best plan of approaching these game birds. His opinion
was sufficient, and then he cautioned us as to the necessity of
great silence. The reason of this caution was his fear that
some kindly neighbor might get frightened at the noise and
fire a *stern* reminder of mustard seed at us.

After a short walk, during which we took great care to follow out all the precautions, we arrived at the bank of an old quarry, at the bottom of which could be seen a series of ponds of crystal waters, reflecting in their bosoms the star-lit canopy of heaven. In one of these small lakes, ruffling this lovely picture, was a flock of richly-plumed birds. They were unconscious of the danger that was approaching so near them.

The banks, with a jagged decline on all sides, approached the water's edge. Led by the "GENERAL," we quickly descended into the hunting grounds. HARRY PAYNE was left on the bank to keep watch and give us timely warning of the approach of anything that might disturb our sport.

We were at the water's edge, the ducks were surrounded; "GENERAL" ordered each man to get a stone. Then all was silence. But at the word we poured a destructive shower of stones upon the unconscious birds, which made a terrible splash. The frightened ducks gave vent to all the vocal power they possessed. Every dog in the neighborhood, awakened by this noise, made the air ring with their fiendish howls. Another storm of stones followed the first, and, if possible, the noise increased. At this period a man was seen on the edge of one of the banks, which frightened all the party. BRADISH yelled out, "A man!" and in less time than it would take to tell it, the quarry was destitute of all life save that contained in the half-dead ducks.

LONEY started across the field at a hundred-yard dash, closely followed by BRADISH, who in his turn had LANDON at his heels. LONEY thought BRADISH was the man after him, and BRADISH thought the same of LANDON, whereas LANDON was frightened at his own shadow. There is no telling how far they would have run, had not BRADISH been brought to a sudden stop by tripping on a cornstalk. As he hit the ground with a heavy thump, he said, "Go on, LONEY—save yourself; I am caught." FRANK stopped to see who had caught "JOHN BULL," and to render all the assistance he could, when, much to the delight of all three, they discovered their mistake.

McDermont and Bradley were not quite so fortunate, for they actually were chased. As they ran by a gate, a man, half dressed, but who was armed with a stick, jumped out at them, but missing his mark, he entered in hot pursuit. All the dogs in the neighborhood, who by this time were wide awake, joined in the chase. Over fences, through fields, across ditches they ran until they came to the Base Ball fence, which Bradley and Mc. vaulted and left their fatigued pursuers on the other side. Breathless and angry, the vanquished man, muttering to himself, slowly returned home.

"General" Myers had from some prominent fence-post taken in at one glance the whole affair, and when he saw this man, accompanied by all the dogs in the neighborhood, start off after Mc. and Bradley, he quickly gathered his scattered band together, and taking advantage of the absence of the enemy, we gathered into the pillow-case all the dead and dying ducks we could lay hands on. This mighty pouch was thrown across our shoulders, and with our plunder we marched through Jugtown into Princeton by the main street, for we felt there was no danger now, as all was quiet and *Morpheus* reigned supreme.

We went to Bradley's room, where we ended the slaughter. The half-dead ducks were taken from the game-bag, one at a time, and beheaded with an old dull knife. They were then hung out of the window in order that they might bleed.

By the light of the early morning, as we were returning from our fruitless attempt at the fly-wheel of the organ, we saw long streaks of blood down the side of the house. Fearing this would reveal our deed, we worked from that time until broad daylight to remove these tracks.

The next evening these ducks were served up in the most approved style, with cider and cigarettes.

McGINNESES' SPECS.

The pair of gilded spectacles which hung in front of a certain book-store, to show to all new-comers that an optician held sway within, had been for many years eagerly sought after by each incoming class, but so carefully did the owner guard his sign that all attempts to obtain it had been fruitless. It was almost an impossible task to try for them, for every evening, as dusk set in, the specs were unhung and housed within the store. Some of us with eagerness had watched its disappearance each night, and notwithstanding the many difficulties we had to surmount, we discussed plans of every character concerning it, but our plans thus far amounted to nothing more than plans. We began to fear that our fate would be the same as that of all other Freshman classes. As this thought grew on us each day the more determined we became. One evening as McDermont, Bradley, Bradford and another happened by the store, they spied the spectacles swinging on the bar.

Now was our chance! now or never!—and heedless of the crowd that was on the street, " John Bull " jumped on Mc.'s shoulders and plucked the glasses from the bar that they had for so many years graced. Before anybody knew what was going on, " John " was half way to his room with the specs snugly tucked under his arm, and in a few hours after it hung as an ornament on his walls.

FRESH FIRE.

Among the annual performances of each Freshman class is that of building a fire around the cannon, and to prove that we could do as much as any other class had ever done, we made all due arrangements necessary to make the attempt a successful one.

In our prospecting for this and other pieces of mischief, we found that the campus contained too many watchmen to allow the building of our fire unmolested, We noticed that at nine o'clock the watchmen were occupied with the task of ringing the bell—at least, one of them held the lamp for another to see to pull the rope in the belfrey, and the third looked on to see that everything was done properly; thus, in the distribution of labor, they left the campus free. That, therefore, was the hour chosen by us to have our illumination.

A few days before the one agreed upon to have our fire we were occupied in collecting fuel. We bought enough coal-oil to set a house on fire, and with this we saturated the boxes and barrels which we had collected.

On the appointed evening we met together at half-past eight, behind a fence which then stood between Clio and Whig Halls. Each man had brought his contributions, which made the atmosphere heavy with the *perfumes of coal-oil.* Two of the party, "SLEEPY" and "GENERAL," were chosen as guards, to give the alarm if any of the watchmen should by accident approach us. All was settled by five minutes of nine, at which time the fellows with their fuel passed over the fence to be ready for the advance as nine o'clock struck. As the first stroke of the ninth hour pealed forth from the old clock in "North," we gathered up our boxes and barrels and started across the campus for the cannon. On our way, "BABE" MONTGOMERY stepped into a hole and rolled headforemost over his barrel. TOMMY BRADFORD was close behind him, and not seeing the mishap of " BABE," he also put his foot in the same hole, and in his attempt to keep himself from falling he stumbled over " BABE," who was by this time picking himself up, and they both rolled over on the ground. The barrels coming together made a terrible noise. Fortunately, at this point the bell began to ring, and drowned all noises made by us. Each man placed his contribution around the cannon. When the last box was placed on the pile we found that it was higher than our heads. When all was ready, " PILL " GILDER threw an extra bucket of oil upon this mass, which so permeated the pores of the wood that only one match was used in igniting it. The match was applied. Immediately the flames leaped high into the air, and by its light could be seen all the fellows running as fast as their legs could carry them, and yelling " *Fire!*" at the top of their lungs, which was sufficiently loud to be heard above the clamor of the bell. The sight of the flames and the sound of the noise we made, awakened the watchmen to their sense of duty. They came rushing around the corner of North but, as usual, a little too late. " MAT " came leisurely out of his office, and after a few words of rebuke to the careless watchmen, he attempted to subdue the flames. His efforts were fruitless, for the mass had grown too warm to allow him to approach near it. At every fruitless attempt he made to " snatch some burning brand from the flames," the whole college, who by this time had turned out to see the fire, would rend the air with cheers and taunt him with jeering remarks, such as " Spit on it!" " Blow it out!" &c.

After some time the fire exhausted its fury, and as it gradually died out, the fellows, returning to their rooms, pronounced it the best fire that any class had had for years.

Satisfied that we had shown the college we were able to do as much as any other Freshman class had done in this line, it became our ambition to surpass any efforts that had ever been made. To this end we entered upon a deeply-laid scheme for building a fire on the top of North College. The work of collecting the materials had begun, and all necessary plans for making this project a successful one had been duly arranged. There is no doubt but that this would have been a grand success, and we certainly would have " astonished the natives," had not an unforeseen accident happened to some of the fellows, which compelled them to leave town for a *short* while. Thus our plan fell through, for those in the party who remained in college did not have the heart or desire to carry the idea into effect.

CHAPTER VII.

HAZING. ·

Discussions, like small streams, are first begun,
Scarce seen they rise, but gather as they run. — *Garth*.

The historian of '80 has made a few remarks upon the subject of hazing which might appear in another light when viewed from another standpoint, and we consider it our duty as members of the class of '81 to view this subject from another position.

He (the historian) admits that although the severity of hazing had almost entirely died away, still the practice had not by any means moderated. This we draw from the numerous accounts he gives of the occurrence of that practice in his own class.

Although the visits of the Sophs. to the members of our class were numerous, no murmur was made by us as long as they did nothing derogatory to the dignity of a gentleman, and although we were Freshmen, that was no reason why we were not to be treated like gentlemen.

As the historian makes much of precedent, we will simply say that it has always been the custom in the annals of colleges to do all their hazing during the first term.

As long as these restrictions were complied with nothing was said against the nocturnal visits of the Sophs. to our class.

We had entered well upon our second term of college life, and considered that we had been duly initiated into the mystery of that life, when to our surprise we found that we were mistaken.

About the middle of February, our class one morning was startled by the news that on the night before "Isty" Lang had by some underhand means been decoyed into the clutches of the Sophs., and had been treated with indecency.

He not only had complied with their requests when asked to give vent to his highly musical voice by putting forth in song, poems of the ancient masters, but he did this gladly; when asked to whistle, he modestly remarked that he could not whistle as well as he could sing," but cheerfully gave them some lively tunes; when music lost its charm to soothe the savage ear he showed the gracefulness of his movements by dancing a jig, and to show their ingratitude they put him through some performances that are entirely out of the line of hazing, and which—I will refrain from narrating.

They ended the evening's entertainment by compelling "Isty" to sign a paper, not what is found in the history of '80, but somewhat different. This note was a slander upon the class of '81. These combined insults were too much for the high spirits of some of our classmen. We might have, through much exertion, been able to swallow these insults had not Carter and Atterbury taunted some of us with the sayings, "that they could haze any man in our class, and that there were none of us who would dare to mention it;" "nor would we dare to resent this insult in any way."

This was bad enough even from a man that had withstood the trials of Freshman year, but coming from a fresh Sophomore, a man that was too timid to pass through the trials of the first year of the course, this was too much. So "Dinks," Hutchings, McDermont, Loney and another intended to initiate Mr. Atterbury and prove the validity of his statements.

We intended to ask Ed. Mathews to join us, but found that he had joined another party who were contemplating the same expedition. After a few consultations, it was determined to join forces and haze Carter at the same time; so Harry Mathews, Bradford, Bradley, Shaw and Flick, added to the six men previously mentioned, became the party.

Monday, February the 18th, was the night settled upon to haze these men. On that evening, after a lecture given by Dr. OTIS, we made our advances in the form of a visit to the two "*gallant Sophomores*" (?) We, however, only numbered ten men, as LANDON was called from town that day, and we were deprived of his cool, deliberate and firm judgment.

Masked, as is the custom in hazing, we ten, having previously found means through which we would find CARTER in ATTERBURY'S room, advanced to the latter's door. On knocking, it was opened by the occupant of the room, who, upon seeing the masked faces, showed his surprise at this unexpected visit (we say unexpected, for some one has said they knew of our proposed visit, and had accordingly loaded their pistols with blank cartridges or soap.)

Upon entering the room, ATTERBURY was thrown upon the floor by LONEY, and CARTER was handled in the same way by BRADFORD. They, since our entrance, had kept up a terrible cry for "Help!" "Murder!" or whatever else that would be most likely to bring forth assistance; but this noise we soon hushed by simply muffling the sounds with our hands. We loosely bound their hands with small cords in order to keep them from doing anything violent. We then produced a paper and read it to them. The following is a copy:

"We, the two members of the party that insulted LANG, and forced him to sign a paper that contained insults against the class of '81, are sorry for what we have done, and do apologise for whatever else we have done against this class."

We told them to place their names to the paper, but ATTERBURY declined, and CARTER, fearing to sign it without its containing the former's signature, also declined.

We threatened CARTER with the extermination of the pride of his life (*his whiskers*) if he did not comply with our wish. We saw him grow pale, but still he refused. Accordingly, we began to reap the growth of years.

ATTERBURY did not have even a growth of down upon his face, so we were compelled to administer, with a paddle of slender white pine, not an allopathic dose, as has been said, but simply a stern reminder. This not having the desired effect, we cut from their heads some of its profuse growth of hair; but this also failed to bring forth the signature, and fearing our visit might become tiresome to the "*demi-gods they felt themselves to be*," we left them bound each to an end of the table, not gagged, as has been said. ATTERBURY, promising not to make any sounds of alarm, we left unmuffled, but CARTER refusing to make this promise, we simply covered his mouth with a handkerchief and, when this was done, bade them good evening.

We had scarcely reached the ground floor when heavy thumps on the front door were heard, and from the upper part of the building we heard the report of two pistol shots, which showed that there was life in that quarter. We retired from the back door, and through the fields towards Chambers street, where we intended going to McDERMONT's room, but changed our minds and passed the house.

We had not gone far, before two figures were seen behind us, and we soon saw, by the light of the moon, that these were none other than our late hosts, who had recognized McDERMONT, and had been to his room to demand an apology, but of course had not found him at home. We, not wishing to be recognized by them, quickened our pace into a run, when we were surprised, startled and alarmed by hearing the reports of two pistol shots, and at almost the same time two bullets were heard to pass some of our heads too close for convenience (but these pistols it is said were loaded with blank cartridges). When we reached the corner by the University Hotel, one of the party, whose name I will not mention, and only one, who happened that evening to have been through a lonely road, had a pistol with him, and for the safety of himself and friends returned the fire. The second of his shots struck ATTERBURY. We had not *cowardly* armed ourselves for that evening, but by accident one of the party happened to be armed.

We then retired to BRADLEY's room, on the top floor of Witherspoon, where, with shaded light, we talked over the possibility of ATTERBURY's being seriously hurt. On our way to Witherspoon, however, we, by the light of the moon, were recognized by some of the members of the faculty, who, on hearing the reports of the pistols, had rushed to their windows to see if they could learn the cause.

The next day the campus was all excitement. Men hurried to and fro, told each other in a whisper of the night's proceedings, and then passed on. Sophomores scowled and turned pale with anger, but the Freshmen chuckled with delight.

Things, by evening, had taken a more serious aspect than we had anticipated when we entered upon this project. It was reported that the town authorities were after the parties who did the shooting, and that the faculty had determined to do everything to find out the men implicated.

The ten concerned, thought it best to have some unity of action, and fearing if we met together in any of our rooms it might be the means of revealing to some lurking spy the party in question, we agreed, when night set in, to meet on the bridge near the Prep. and discuss our future movements.

There, by a rippling stream, under the broad canopy of heaven, and in the light of the silver moon, we held our meeting.

After some discussion, it was determined to acknowledge everything, if questioned by the faculty, and take the consequences.

We had just returned home, when one of the party received a formal summons to appear before the faculty, which he immediately complied with, and answered, in as accurate a manner as was within his power, all questions put to him.

On his return to the room, where the fellows were anxiously awaiting his arrival, he told them some of the questions and answers he had received and given. Then he said, "There was one of them, who was very large, had big feet, and was very deliberate in his conversation, whose name I do not know—he tried to make me lie, but could not."

PORTLY PROFESSOR.—"Had you any implements of torture?"

FRESHMAN.—"That depends, Sir, upon what you call an implement of torture. Would you call a paddle an implement of torture?"

PROFESSOR.—"I certainly should."

FRESHMAN.—"Then, Sir, we certainly had."

PROFESSOR.—"What were the character and dimensions of this paddle, and had it any spikes in it?"

The minute details as to the shape, size and material of the paddle were given by the Freshman, who closed his answer with the fact that this implement of torture contained nothing that even resembled spikes, nor did it have holes in it.

After a few more such questions, the worthy Professor stated the fact that the answers had been satisfactory, as he had seen the paddle himself.

After narrating a few more of the incidents of the cross-examination, it was determined that seven of the ten should remain together in one room that night, as we heard the Sophomores intended to give us a "surprise party," and we knew it would be more sociable if we all *received* together. We, however, were disappointed, for they overlooked us and paid their respects to JUDGE STRONG, who, however, had a canine friend acting as porter, and who behaved so rudely to them in his sullen bull-dog manner that they concluded not to stay that evening, but would call some other evening. Good evening!

The next morning we were officially informed that the faculty had determined to suspend us indefinitely, and we must leave town before the next morning. We, however, were informed that afternoon that the civil authorities were after us, and that we had better leave town as quietly as possible.

This we did. With scarcely time to take a collar or a pair of cuffs, we started off for the Junction in twos, threes, or alone. When finally we arrived at the Junction, a telegram was received by SHAW, which stated that the whole of the Soph. class was coming down after us. This was anything but pleasant news. We had but little time to make up our minds as to the best plan of action. It was wonderful how many plans were proposed and discussed in so short a space of time. SHAW wanted to run to Trenton—a distance of only ten miles; FLICK wanted to take to the woods; but these plans were all squelched. The majority agreed to get clubs and stand our ground. This we did, and in this attitude of defence we were found when the train from Princeton came thundering up, puffing under the load of Sophomores which it brought.

On they came, about eighty-five in number, and firmly we stood, determined to hold our position until our train came in. But "MAT" came to our assistance, and hustled us into one corner of the waiting-room, while he kept guard at the door until the train for Philadelphia arrived. So loud was the yell of the Sophs. that the whistle of the train could scarcely be heard.

"MAT" with his club an opening made, and through this howling body of Sophs. we passed. It has been stated that nothing was thrown at us, at the station. This is a mistake, for the writer for one has the feeling recollection of having been hit in the back of the head by some missile. We, however, reached the train without any broken limbs, and when the train moved off we sat down with more ease than we had experienced for some time.

FLICK stretched out his feet (which, I must say, are quite large) and struck something, he knew not what, when, much to his surprise, he saw a human head appear from under the seat ; then came a white cravat. The wearer of this article asked in a trembling voice, " Is it all over?" " Is what all over?" asked FLICK. " I mean," said the minister (for such was his profession), " is there any danger now? Have we passed Princeton?" " Oh, yes," said FLICK, " you can come out now with safety." The minister came from his hiding-place and sat in the seat by FLICK, but all the while kept one eye on him.

When we arrived in Trenton, a boy came in the cars, making quite a noise calling out "*Nice hot oysters!*" We each bought a box to appease the gnawings of hunger, but when we stuck our teeth into them we found them not only taste-less but stone cold. We asked the boy why he called them *hot oysters*, and he blandly answered, "Because that was the name of them." With one accord we fired the ten boxes, with their oysters, at his head. This was too much for FLICK's friend, the minister, who immediately left the train.

Nothing more of interest happened until we arrived in Philadelphia, where we remained for the night.

What was our consternation the next morning when we saw our names in full in all the papers, and heard on every corner the newsboy cry, " Terrible Bloodshed in Princeton!" " Open Riot at Princeton!" Others also rent the air with the words, "Full account of the Rowdyism at Princeton!" and many other such headings that appeared in the papers.

This proved an elegant opportunity for the reporters to put before the public their ideas as to what should be done with young men and how they should be treated, and for weeks afterwards they would boil over and write something concerning the affair. But to Princeton it has proved of valuable importance. It gained two ends where only one was intended. We were brought prominently before the public and made Princeton more famous, and also it put a stop to all hazing, for no cases have been heard of since that memorable evening.

CHAPTER VIII.

FOOT BALL.

Our record in foot ball is one that any college might be proud to claim. During the four years of our course, Princeton has not lost a game, and our class has done its share towards making the *orange and black* flutter triumphantly on its many fields of victory.

In Freshman year, LONEY and BRADFORD were chosen on the University team, and two others of our class acted as substitutes.

The numbers of our class on the team increased each year, and made the University more able to hold her head above all other colleges in this sport. In Sophomore year, FRANK LONEY made the only point we scored against Harvard, and one of his plays against Yale that year was the means of gaining us the College championship, which with clear-headed and dexterous playing we have been able to retain ever since. Under the captainship of FRANK LONEY, this year, we resisted successfully the efforts of the strongest team Yale has had in the field for many years, to take the championship from us.

Not only has our class showed to such good advantage on the University, but its own team has won for Princeton laurels of which they may well be proud.

Our team had a series of captains. "JOHN BULL," was first elected to that position, because he was an Englishman and of course knew all about the game. He believed in training the men hard. After our first day's practice, he started off at the head of the team at a brisk run, announcing beforehand that he intended to run to the "Prep." and back. The fellows began at Jugtown to give out, and by the time

"JOHN" got to the "Prep." DAVE RICKETS was the only one of this team that had survived. The fellows sat down on the curb-stone all along the road in order to regain their strength so that they could return home with the team. This run used the fellows up to such an extent that many of them stopped playing because they objected to being killed while training. Because the fellows would not train, "JOHN" took offence and resigned.

CROSBY, who had been chosen as one of the substitutes on the University team, was elected by our class to fill the vacancy caused by the resignation of "JOHN BULL."

Under the more moderate system of training of our second captain the fellows developed considerable skill and pluck in playing. We gained so much confidence in our own ability as foot-ball players, that we challenged the P. L. S. team of New York to play us on the 10th of November, on our grounds. Much to our delight, a few days after our challenge was sent, we received an acceptance.

The team worked hard, and looked with anxious expectation towards the day when they should appear for the first time on the foot-ball field to play a match game.

The memorable tenth at last came, as did the P. L. S. team, but unfortunately a stormy spell of weather had arrived a few days before, and the rain continued to fall in sheets. The consequence was that the grounds were not in a very good condition to play on. As the opposing team had put in an appearance, there was no alternative left us. At the appointed time the two teams made their appearance on the grounds, and after only a few moments' delay every man was in his position. Our team presented a comical appearance. No two men wore the same kind of a costume. TOMMY had on a pair of old pants that have since become very familiar to us, one or two of the fellows wore knee-pants, and most of them had on slouch hats of all descriptions and colors. The canvas jackets which they wore were none the better off for long usage and few washings.

The ball was set in motion by CROSBY, and after it had been kicked a few times from one side of the field to the other, it came to TOMMY, who tucked the *leather* under his arm and started down the field. He had not gone far when he was "tackled" ferociously by one of the P. L. S. "rushers," when TOMMY tried his trick of ducking down and letting the opponent fall over his head, but unfortunately the P. L. S. sat down on TOMMY's head, mashing it into the mud. When he succeeded in extricating his buried member out of the soft mud, his whole face was smeared, his eyes and mouth full of mud, and his whole body streaked and spattered with dirt. He was the first one who had fallen, but before the game was ended the same fate had happened to each of us, and we all looked alike; notwithstanding the varied costumes we started the game in, we all left the field with a *muddy brown* hue.

On account of the difficulty we found in running on this slippery surface, we only made a score of two goals and five touchdowns.

After we had scraped off the dirt and changed our football costume for a more cleanly suit, we gathered around the festive board and had a social meal together. During the repast each team complimented the other on the many fine plays they made. We received their congratulations with smiles, because we were perfectly satisfied with the score under the circumstances, and felt much encouraged with our playing, for the P. L. S. had won for themselves in New York, the name of being fine players.

They returned to New York that evening, and we, fatigued and sore from the day's exertions, retired early, to dream of victories on the foot-ball field. We know this was the subject of some of the dreams, because ED. MATHEWS kicked HARRY out of bed while dreaming that he was kicking the ball.

Soon after this game a sad accident happened to CROSBY. While we were practicing, back of Reunion, some man accidentally kicked him in the back of the head, while the latter in a "*tackle*" was thrown upon the ground. So violent was this blow that CROSBY lay for some time motionless upon the ground. Stimulants had no effect upon him, and by the time medical assistance was obtained he showed some signs of delirium. He was carried to his room, where for many days he lay tossing in wild unconsciousness. The doctor entertained serious apprehensions that CROSBY's symptoms might prove to be congestion of the brain. He fortunately, after a prolonged illness, recovered, but his health was so much impaired that he was compelled to leave college.

Another member of the team was elected to fill his place. Under the new captain, challenges were sent to Yale and Harvard Freshmen. They, however, were not able to play us. Arrangements were made to play the customary game with Lawrenceville. The day agreed upon by both parties was the 21st of November, and to be played on their grounds.

This game proved the hardest and most exciting one that our class team ever played. The teachers of the school made up a very strong portion of their team. They played a much rougher game than we had anticipated, and at first we did not know exactly how to treat them.

The game had just started, and the ball had not long been put in motion, when "Judge" STRONG, in making a desperate "tackle," ran his nose violently against his opponent's arm. The "Judge's" injured member bled profusely for a short time, long enough to compel him to stop playing. He was led, bleeding, from the field, and his position filled by the first substitute. The ball was soon put in motion again, and was followed closely as it was kicked from one side of the field to the other. Our team, urged on by the captain, worked hard to score something in the first half. We struggled in this way until within two minutes of the end of the first half. At this period McDERMONT seized the ball, which was well down by our goal, and made a beautiful run beyond the middle of the field. Here he was "tackled," but passed the ball to LONEY, who started down the field at the top of his speed. The first man that attempted to stop him only succeeded in retaining the sleeve of his jacket; the next man also fell short of his mark and got his hand in the neck of Loney's shirt, but this gave way and was torn from his back, thus leaving him with only a thin undershirt to cover his body, but still he ran on, and the ball was fast approaching their goal line. There was but one more man to pass, while at Loney's heels both teams came bolging down. The goalkeeper, when he saw the fruitless attempts of the other men of his team in trying to stop Loney, planted his feet more steadily and made one desperate effort. It was too late; Loney bore him behind the goal-posts and touched the ball down. We did not have time to try for a goal, for *time* was almost immediately called. We thus scored our first touchdown, but in the struggle Loney had lost two shirts, which were replaced by others during the intermission. During the second half of the game we scored another touchdown, but Tommy Cauldwell failed to kick a goal from it. This game was the last one our team played in Freshman year. We had a good record; had beaten every game we played, and had not had anything scored on us.

The men that played most on the team, and who had their pictures taken to represent '81 in this sport, were Bradish, Bradford, Brown, Cauldwell, Farr, Landon, Loney, McAlpin, McDermont, Monroe, Ed. Mathews, Rickets, A. Scribner, and Strong.

When we returned to College Sophomore year, the captain who had succeeded Crosby resigned his position, and Landon was elected in his place, thus making the fourth captain we had had in just one year. Landon arranged a game with the Columbia Sophomores, to be played in Hoboken on the Saturday after Thanksgiving.

The day was clear, and the fellows were in good condition and spirits. After a short delay the fellows took their positions. Our team consisted of the following eleven men: The *rushers* were Landon (captain), Bradford, McDermont,

McAlpin, Roberts, and A. Scribner; the half backs were Farr, Allen, and Loney, while the two backs were Cauldwell and Lowrie. At about half-past two the captain of the Columbia team kicked off the ball, and it did not take long for us to see that Columbia had determined to play entirely on the defensive. It took Landon just fourteen minutes to make the first touchdown, from which Cauldwell kicked a goal. From this instant it was only a question of time as to how large a score we would make. A few minutes after the ball had been kicked off Frank Allen got hold of it, and ran the whole length of the field, warding off men, and finally crossed the goal line, and made the second touchdown. The third was also made by him, and in four minutes after the ball was brought out Loney made the fourth touchdown, but not before he had accidentally been hit in the mouth, which caused a profuse flow of blood. Just at the end of the first half of the game another touchdown was made, but was not allowed. Soon after we had started the second half of the game, "Tommy" got hold of the ball and started down the field; although a number of the Columbia team called out to each other to stop him, still none of them succeeded in doing so until just before he reached the goal line, when he was desperately "tackled" by one of their *backs*. "Tommy," however passed the ball to Frank Loney, who ran in and touched it down. In four minutes after the ball was put in play again Landon secured another touchdown. About this time "Powers" hurt himself, and Greer Monroe was put on in his place. In a short while, after Landon made his touchdown, Scribner made another, which was followed in quick succession by two other touchdowns by another member of the team.

Columbia was perfectly demoralized (as they well might have been), and when the game was ended the score stood six goals and ten touchdowns to nothing; this being the largest score up to that date that had ever been made in a match game. This overwhelming victory closed the series of games played by our class in foot ball.

CHAPTER IX.

CLASS MEETINGS.

Many are the pleasant features of a college class meeting ; many the causes for which they are called, and varied the ideas put forth in them. The flash of wit and sparkling repartee have often made hours that would have proved dull and heavy pass most pleasantly, and prove the most enjoyable in our course. To mention the meetings called for boating, base ball, and foot ball, would be useless, and a waste of time. A few of our gatherings, however, deserve a notice in this history.

On the 22d of September, 1877, our first meeting was called for the election of officers. After many nominations we succeeded in electing a man to each of the offices on record ; when this was done, and there seemed to be nothing to prevent us from adjourning, MIKE O'RIAN rose and said— "Mr. President! It is now in order to transact business." All eyes were turned upon the speaker. He was a man short in statue, thickly built, and having the appearance of being a descendant of Ireland. To us he appeared well advanced in years ; we therefore sat in silence, listening to what wise counsel he would give us.

After a prelude, he informed the president that a committee should be appointed to draw up a constitution for the class. If we did not have one, said he, everything we would do will be illegal, and *therefore* we could not do anything.

We had heard enough, and set up an unearthly howl, which so bewildered this worthy gentleman that he sat down. He was *squelched ;* this is the only time on record that MIKE O'RIAN was ever quieted.

The second meeting of importance was held the 8th of January, 1879. This was called to discuss the feasibility of having a " Sophomore Reception." Much opposition was expected from those who wanted a class supper, or even the old burial which had been the exercise with which many Sophomore years had been brought to a triumphant close.

Before the meeting was called, a number who were in favor of the " Reception " gathered together. After a little discussion eight or nine men were appointed to get up in succession in different parts of the room, and speak in favor of the motion. This scheme worked beautifully, all nine men spoke without any interruption except applause. One speech was made against it. The motion, that we would have a reception, was then put, and carried by a large majority.

Without further delay the committee for arrangements was elected, and the meeting adjourned.

Another occasion of much importance was that protracted meeting held for the election of " PRINCETONIAN" and " LIT " editors.

During this meeting much talking was done, all the argumentative force of the class was brought to bear. The men who are to be eminent in the future made themselves conspicuous on this occasion. " BONNER " SKINNER (for instance) made several eloquent and enthusiastic orations ; after speaking several times, he rose again to harangue the audience. Some one objected to his speaking so often, whereupon "BONNER" asked permission of the house to speak again, and went on to say in his modest manner, that he had nothing of importance to say, but—at this point " DUFF " jumped up and said, " If the gentleman has nothing of importance to say, I move he let some one else speak." BONNER was *sat upon*, just because he was a little modest. He learned from this occasion that modesty was not his method, and has not been troubled in that way since.

The important meeting held for the election of class day offices proved to be an occasion that will long be remembered by the members of '81 with satisfaction and mirthfulness. The " wire pulling " that has been the characteristic of many previous class-day elections was entirely omitted by us. Three of the most important offices were elected unanimously, and little rivalry was found in the petty offices, but when the nomination for class-day committee was in order, nearly every man in the class rose simultaneously to nominate a friend. They by degrees crowded around the chairman's desk, and stood there until they, in their turn, had been recognized by him. The number of nominations for this committee exceeded fifty. When quiet was restored the balloting began and continued until we adjourned for dinner; at three o'clock the balloting was reopened.

The time spent in counting the votes had become tiresome, the different characteristics of the men were shown in the amusements they sought to pass away the time. DIX sat reading a novel; VAN ALLEN, DICK HARLAND, KIMBLE, CRAVEN and DODD were playing a game of " draw poker." McCUNN and " DUFF " were poaling the new base ball rules; VANDEBURGH was poaling his lesson in " Dadd " for the next day. Thus all were occupied, but seemed weary. Suddenly DAVE WILLS arose and made the welcome announcement that a member of our class would restore our drooping minds with refreshing music.

Often the choicest talents are hidden beneath the veil of modesty, and when this mantle is withdrawn by the hand of chance, we have revealed to us a gem of the first water.

This meeting revealed to us a talent which had been hidden for more than three years. Oh! lucky meeting! had it never been held, the world would have missed a songster and we a treat.

DAVE WILLS, who had often heard the sweet strains of " Mother Orr's " voice, penetrating the stone partition that separated their rooms, prevailed upon " Mother " to give vent to some of his high, full, sweet notes in *original* music, and it was for this purpose that he now asked the attention of the class. He said, in his neat little introductory speech, that he knew we would find in these songs some of the sweetest notes ever sounded by man (for " Mother Orr " is known to be a man).

The first piece started :

> " I'm a gay trall-a-la,
> I'm a gay trall-a-lu," &c.

The music original of course. He reminded us more of the pictures seen of ancient bards, pouring forth their souls in sweet music at the foot-stool of some haughty queen, than anything it had ever been our good fortune to have seen before. The expression of his face, was enough to have inspired anyone. His eyebrows elevated, his eyes upraised spoke pleading words of sweetness. The expression about the mouth was something grand, his lips quivered with emotion, At times he entered so deeply into the feeling of the song that the rosy tint which mantled his velvety cheek would die away into an ashy pallor.

When the echoes of his last silvery note was no longer audible, we broke the stillness with appreciative applause. So ardent and lengthened was this request for a repetition of his musical talent, that with blushes and bows of modesty he rose and announced that the next song would also be a sad, sweet strain, put to music by himself. He was afraid (said he) that he could not do it justice, for his *cold* was so bad he could not strike some of its highest notes clearly. It was to be sung in a falsetto voice. He got through his song without much detriment to his *bald* spot or his nose, and received hearty applause for his trouble and exertion. He gained more confidence in his abilities, so much, in fact, that he *volunteered* to deliver, " as it should be done," Poe's Bells. He mentioned, as a passing remark, that he would have to fill in parts as he went along, because his memory failed him.

After he had ended a successful rendering of this piece our attention was drawn to the results of the voting, and we left for the present, the *bard*, *poet*, and *orator*, all in one.

CHAPTER X.

JUNIOR YEAR·

The year which is usually the period of luxury, ease and mirth, was in our course peculiarly sad and uneventful. It was begun under sad auspices and ended with the same.

One of the most appreciable events of the first term of this year was the inability of Prof. BRACKEN to give us an examination in that light subject, Physics, and that portion especially was dreaded which was so thoroughly touched upon by "CUMMINGS." This he announced to us at the end of the last recitation for the first term. At this joyous news the fellows flew down stairs yelling at the top of their voices, many went through touching scenes of congratulation, as a means of expressing the joy they felt on this occasion.

During the first and second term a few *spreads* were given by the most generous of the class. The givers were prompted to these feasts by different desires and motives. The new-comers thought this a good way to become acquainted with, and pick from them, men with whom they were to associate for the next two years, any who might happen to show their *blue blood* at the feast. Others intended the banquet as a peace-maker and to clear up old scores, for they believed in the saying that a man's heart is touched through his stomach. Others, however, gave their spreads with no other avowed intention than to have a good time. No matter what the motive was that prompted each giver to such acts of generosity, they all proved enjoyable affairs.

Not having space to describe all, and not wishing to detract from the grandeur of any, your historian feels a delicacy in selecting for description the one that might suit his esthetic nature, but has deemed it improper to allow the following to pass without notice.

PLINY FISK one afternoon came around to a few of his friends and told them in his confidential way that he was going to have a little spread in his room that evening, and after assuring them of the informality of the occasion, asked them to come about half-past eight.

Promptly at the appointed hour, the fellows who previously had been asked entered PLINY'S room, and expected to see the table decorated with handsome china, but much to their surprise they saw something resembling a bowl, which stood alone upon the table, and was neatly covered with a towel. PAUL VAN DYKE thought it was a punch bowl, and told PLINY in a whisper that he never drank before the fellows, and especially the crowd that was in the room, but just to save him some and he would come in when the fellows were not there. This request made PLINY fear that the fellows expected too much, therefore he said: "Fellows! I have not much to offer you, but I guess what there is of it is pretty strong." "Yes," whispered PAUL, "I like it strong;" and then he gave PLINY a meaning wink. At this instant the towel was withdrawn, and much to the horror of the assembled body, they saw a very familiar piece of china. PLINY asked the fellows to pitch in and not be bashful, and said the contents of the bowl was a new kind of cheese called a *potifull* cheese, he said it was recommended very highly. He finally announced that he had some crackers and water to go with it if any of the fellows wanted any. All the time that he had been talking he was working away at the cheese with his knife. No one made answer to his kind invitation. PAUL'S chin had dropped as soon as the towel was lifted and now his face was darkened by the deepest shades of disappointment.

BRUCE had not eaten any supper that evening in order that he might do justice to PLINY'S spread, and now he did not relish the idea of the alternative left him, which was to fast until morning, or feast on this *potifull* cheese. He finally took a handful of crackers with a small pinch of cheese. The rest of the fellows, by degrees, followed BRUCE's example, but it did not take long to satisfy them, and by half-past nine the door closed behind the last visitor.

At the end of a week BLYDENBURGH stook scraping the last few crumbs into his hand; PLINY put on one of his *dry grins* and said : "That certainly was a success, eh, BLYDEN? My spread beat PHIL JACKSON's by five days."

Another feast was held by BILLY BACOT one evening towards the end of the second term in this year. A chosen few, alone, were invited to this *liquid* spread, and among this number CRAVEN could be seen. After the fellows had all arrived BILLY brought in a large bowl of punch which he had previously prepared, and much to the surprise of all present CRAVEN accepted a bumper when offered him and drained the mug without changing a muscle of his face, after storing away three or four glasses of punch and smoking a package of cigarettes he asked for another glass of " raspberry sauce." His face grew red with blushes and his head hung upon his breast with shame when he found that he had been drinking real punch, while he thought that it was nothing but " raspberry sauce." Soon after CRAVEN learnt, what a mistake he had made, he took his departure and as the punch was all gone, the other guests soon followed his example. Finally BILLY was left alone with but one guest. They were both drowsy (because it was late), but BILLY was not too sleepy to make a pun or two which he took note of for his department of the " Lit." Finally some fellow called out in an agonized tone of voice : "Hello, PORTER," immediately BILLY's face brightened, and after an *audible* smile he made the following play on PORTER's name : " That fellow must be sick and is crying for some sort of stimulus. I can't *bear* the sound of his voice, I would like to know what *ails* him." BILLY's drowsy friend made no signs of recognition, but BILLY continued : " It makes me tired to see such sparkling effervescence of *sham-pain* escape without meeting with a more *cordial* welcome." This was too much for the visitor who suddenly disappeared from the room.

In the middle of the second term as we approached the end of our course in logic, DAD announced to us that his examination, which had formerly taken place in the mid term had been postponed by the faculty until the end of the term. This news was as grievous to us as the announcement of the omission of the examination in physics in the first term had been pleasing. Most of the fellows were anxious to get through with it while the subject was clear in their minds, and a petition was sent to the faculty requesting them to allow us to have the examination at the customary time. This petition was granted and the examination passed, but the spree which usually follows the *final in logic* was omitted. Because the faculty had granted our request, not even CHARLEY RYLE and his noisy gang made as much fuss on the evening which followed the examination as was their custom at other times.

This year was brought to an untimely close by the appearance of malarial fever, which proved so fatal in some cases. On account of this fever no junior finals were even passed by us.

IN MEMORIA.

" As in Adam all die, so in Christ shall all be made alive again."

A few days after our return to College, in junior year, the veil of sadness was cast upon all the members of the class of '81 by hearing of the death of REUBEN LOWRIE. His abilities in gaining scholastic honors had won for him our highest respect and the success which he had gained in athletic sports had added our unbounded admiration to the other features of highest love. His death was deeply felt by every member of the class, and we grieved his loss with heart felt sadness.

The following resolutions were drawn up by the class and hall to which he belonged :

PRINCETON, Sept. 11, 1879.

Whereas, It has pleased Almighty God in His infinite wisdom to take unto Himself our beloved classmate and brother REUBEN LOWRIE ; and

Whereas, In his death the class of 1881, feel the loss of our honored and esteemed member ; therefore

Resolved, That we, his classmates, extend to his afflicted family our sincerest sympathy in this our common bereavment ;

Resolved, That the members of the class wear a badge of mourning for thirty days ; and

Resolved, That a copy of these resolutions be sent to his family and be inserted in the *Princeton Press, Nassau Literary Magazine* and the *Princetonian.*

In behalf of the class.

H. J. DUFFIELD,
JOHN L. KIRK,
J. O. H. PITNEY,
Committee.

Hall of the American Whig Society,
Sept. 12, 1879.

Whereas, It has pleased God in His all-wise providence to move from our number REUBEN LOWRIE, of the class of 1881 ; therefore,

Resolved, That, although, the American Whig Society is truely sensible of the loss of a worthy and beloved member, we recognize in this event the will of One who doeth all things well.

Resolved, That our heartfelt sympathy is tended to the bereaved mother and friends, for their loss we can ourselves appreciate.

Resolved, That a copy of these resolutions be sent to the family, and also be published in the *Nassau Literary Magazine* and the *Princetonian.*

R. D. HARLAND,
T. D. WARREN,
Committee.

During the fever which sadly closed our junior year, our much loved classmate, IRWIN B. SCHULTZ, was struck down, During his illness he showed a true Christian spirit, was submissive to the will of an all-wise Providence, was thoughtful of the feelings of others and considerate in all things After a prolonged illness, his doctor one morning found that he could not recover, and cautiously imparted this sad news to him. He did not appear unaware of his condition, but in his weak, trembling voice murmured a few appropriate prayers, and peacefully his spirit passed away; no struggle disturbed his last moments; no pangs of conscience made him afraid to die, but so quietly did he draw his last breath that no one knew when it came. This was a fit ending for as true a follower of Christ, as he in all his actions had shown himself to be.

The following resolutions indicative of the grief felt throughout College caused by his death were drawn up by the class and hall of which he was member :

PRINCETON, Sept. 15, 1880.

Whereas, It has pleased God, who doth all things well, to take home our much loved classmate, IRWIN B. SCHULTZ ; therefore be it

Resolved, That the three years of our fellowship have taught us to feel how feebly resolutions of this nature can express our sorrow, when we mourn one whose generous heart, sunny spirit and Christian character have endeared him to each of us, and whose shining talents gave promise of such noble manhood.

Resolved, That we extend to his bereaved family our heart felt sympathy in their deep affliction.

Resolved, That in token of this our loss, we wear a badge of mourning for thirty days, and that these resolutions be sent to the family, and be published in the *Nassau Literary Magazine*, the *Princetonian*, and the *Boyertown Messenger*.

In behalf of the Class of '81.

> CHAS. G. TITSWORTH,
> CHAS. C. ROBBINS,
> WM. T. VLYMEN,
> T. W. CAULDWELL.

HALL OF THE CLIOSOPHIC SOCIETY.

Whereas, God has seen fit in His unerring Providence to remove, from our brotherhood, by death, IRWIN B. SCHULTZ; and

Whereas, We feel in his death the loss of a sincere friend, a zealous advocate of all that he believed honorable and just, and one whom we all love and esteem because of his manly character; be it

Resolved, That we extend to his grief-stricken family our heartfelt sympathy in our common bereavement; therefore

Resolved, That a copy of these resolutions be sent to his family, and also be published in the *Nassau Literary Magazine*, and the *Princetonian*.

In behalf of the Society,

> CHAS. C. ROBBINS,
> CHAS. C. CRAVEN,
> *Committee.*

Wednesday, the 26th of May, 1880, proved to be a sad day for our class. The cause of this sadness was the death of JAMES P. SHAW, who by his own hand, during the delirium of fever, brought his young life to an untimely end. When the sad news of the accident reached the ears of the fellows, they were struck with horror and consternation, many wandered listlessly about the campus absorbed with their own meditations, others were seen gathered together in small groups, and here talked of the sad affair with subdued voices. Those who visited the room of the sad scene felt extra pangs of sorrow when they saw the blood stained carpet. His death was so sudden and unexpected that it brought vividly before the minds of many the shortness of life, and its unexpected end.

That truly was a sad and restless night for more than one, because death always seems more dreadful when we see a friend snatched from us by an accident than when they peacefully pass away. All was done by our class that could in any way appease the bereaved mother ; but nothing could comfort her. The next day after his death the heart broken mother followed the body of her only son to her western home, and his final resting place.

CHAPTER XI.

A CHAPTER OF ACCIDENTS.

In this article it has been our endeavor to write only such things as happened, and whatever mention is made of the faculty we wish it understood that nothing of a slighting nature is intended, but as historian we considered it our duty to record things as they happened and not as was most pleasing to the ear. The first thing noticed was BILLY INGHAM's visit to PHIL JACKSON's room, which was as follows :

One day BILLY INGHAM picked up in PHIL JACKSON's room a well-worn catalogue, and while he glanced over its pages he noticed a mark after the name of each undergraduate.

"PHIL!" said BILLY, "what do all those marks mean?"
"Oh," said PHIL, as he took his feet from off the table where they had lately been resting, "those names with a dagger after them I call my visiting list; those marked with a cross are men whom I only know to speak to on the street; those followed by a straight mark shows I do not know them, but hope to make their acquaintance soon, and you may have noticed some with stars after their names, those BILLY are men whom I have known, but do not recognize now ; you see they are very few in number." Here his voice assumed a very serious tone, and he said: "Men who have held and expect to hold the offices I have, must know every one they can. I visit every evening." Here BILLY broke in and said, "not that I ever expect to hold any offices, but how long do you generally stay in each fellow's room." PHIL in a very condescending manner went on to say, that when he visited a fellow only once in a while, he generally staid until one or two o'clock in the morning, but in the rooms where he visited oftener, he did not stay quite so late.

"BILLY!" said PHIL, "I have some beautiful cravats I would like to show you, would you not like to see them?" and upon BILLY expressing his willingness to see PHIL's wardrobe, he was forthwith shown a whole drawerful of cravats, glittering with all the colors of the rainbow. PHIL had no less than twenty blue cravats, and almost as many bright red, thirteen mixed, eight orange and black, he also had a few brown ones which he wanted BILLY to take, for he said they were too tame for him and that he would never wear them, and as an extra inducement told BILLY that they would be very becoming to his peculiar style of beauty. This made BILLY a little angry, as he does not like to have his hair mentioned, and in a fretful manner he walked towards the stove; he, however, found not the sign of a living coal in it, and turning to PHIL he said: "Is it not a little cold in this room?' PHIL said, " oh, no, it was not cold then, but he was sorry he had no fire if BILLY was cold, and then he confidentially told him that he was "laying for a drawback," and whenever it became too cold in his room he went in to see VAN, who always had a nice fire and was glad to see him at any time. BILLY in .a short while took his departure, but could not help thinking what a lucky fellow PHIL was, so many friends, such an elegant collection of cravats, and " laying for a drawback."

There is a story told on the Governor, for the truth of which we cannot altogether vouch. It is as follows: One evening while the " Gov." sat thoughtfully looking into the fire, picturing in the dying embers the revelation of sciences unknown and worlds unseen by any but himself, or it may be that he thought of the day to come when he would be proclaimed President of the United States, but whatever his thoughts were, he was disturbed from his meditation by a rap upon the door, which announced, at this time, the unwelcomed arrival of some visitor. Provoked at being disturbed, he in no pleasant mood answered the rap and ushered in a classmate. No sooner had this visitor become well settled than he hurt the sensitive ear of the " Gov." by starting some topic much lighter than the thoughts which he had so lately been pondering over. He could not help showing his annoyance in his face, but his visitor heedlessly rambled on, and by way of making his remarks more impressive he used some mild swear words. At this instant the " Gov.' in his mild way, but with flushed face and flashing eye, said : " Sir ! you will please not again pollute the air of my room with any such remarks."

This had the desired effect, the visitor soon left.

The following episode may show how that letter writing, when done in a hurry, often causes much embarrassment. DOUGALL writes and receives a great many letters. One evening he was expecting a letter from a certain person, and appeared at the post-office at an early hour. His face beamed with smiles when he saw his name upon the slate, but when the letter was handed him he failed to recognize the hand-writing, he hurriedly opened the envelope, and with astonishment read thus :

" MY DEAR HUSBAND : I arrived here in safety this morning, and our dear *baby* is perfectly well ; excuse shortness, am in great haste. Write soon to your loving   MAGGIE."

DOUGALL was so dazed by the unexpected contents of the letter that he showed it to " MOTHER " ORR, and asked him what he had better do about the *letter*. " MOTHER " advised that if there was any mistake, he had better return it to the postmaster. This parental advice he immediately followed, and assured " MOTHER " that it was all a mistake ; it was too good to be smothered, and the next day DOUGALL received many congratulations and a rattle for the baby.

This story was told by one of the following trio :

McMUNDY, BOB WILLIAMS, and FLICK strolled out one clear Sunday afternoon in the third term of Senior year, and while they were walking leisurely along, enjoying the beauties of Nature, their attention was attracted to a modest little building from which came the sweet strains of a Sunday-school in full blast. The three wanderers approached the building and hung around the door for some time, *looking for somebody.* The superintendent came out and invited them in and gave them each a class of small boys to instruct. On their way in FLICK whispered to BOB that there might be a meeting of the teachers after Sunday-school, and that they would stay to it.

They then wasted the hour set apart for instruction in the vain attempt to keep their scholars in order. At the end of this hour the superintendent called upon the teachers to give a text from the Bible on the fool. All had given their text but *the three*, their turn came next, and they were called upon in the following order: BOB WILLIAMS came first, and gave as his text: "Go thou sluggard inquire of the ants." The superintendent deemed a word of explanation necessary to show to the children that a sluggard was often a fool.

Mc was next called upon and said: "As the dog returneth to his vomit, so the fool to his folly." No explanation was necessary.

FLICK arose without being called upon and gave the following as his text: "He that loves wine, women and song, will be a fool his whole life long." Then said it was from St. Matthew, twelfth chapter, and eleventh verse.

They lingered about the door of the little building several Sundays after this, but were never again invited in to teach.

DICK HARLAN, in Junior year, made a contract with a shoemaker to have a pair of shoes *built*. The agreement was that they should be delivered in Princeton for a certain price. After the shoemaker had completed his task he found that he had lost money on them, and in order that he might save as much as possible, sent them by freight, and afterwards grumbled because he did not know that the canal ran so near to their place of destination.

Many amusing incidents have happened in the recitation room during our course, and although they caused much mirth and noise at the time, would fall flat if repeated; a few, however, might cause an audible smile when brought to remembrance. Among these was the mistake made by "Van" in Fresh Year about making a *flock of bees roost* all night on a tree. The many attempts we made in "Cam" to make him get off his *expectorating* joke ; and many others could be mentioned.

Prof. Cam.—Mr. Breckenridge, in honor of whom were the Olympic games celebrated ?

Sleepy.—In honor of Olympus, sir.

Recitation in Political Economy.

Prof. Atwater.—Mr. Brown, if we had a heap of silver dollars what would we do with them ?

Brown.—Set up a dollar store, sir.

Prof. Murry.—Mr. McMundy, to what period does the Elizabethen period belong?

McMundy.—To the age of Elizabeth, sir.

Prof. Rockwood's recitation.

Now I don't want you all to make so much noise when you come into my room. Please close all books and put them under your seats. Mr. Frost, I will not have you marking on my benches, &c.

Recitation in Professor Orris.

One day Powers Farr had not behaved himself with the dignity becoming a man under this grave professor, and for his indecorum was ordered to appear after the recitation to answer for his misconduct. At the appointed time, Powers with drooping head received a long but valuable lecture, and after a word of timely warning, the Professor modulated his loud voice to a subdued tone and gently caught hold of Powers' arm, and with an expressive look said : "my dear young friend do you know the devil has hold of you ? " Powers could not restrain a smile at this startling piece of information, and immediately the Professor saw the mistake he had made but it was too late, he had said it and it was too good a grind to keep quiet, it had its rounds in the papers.

One day while reciting in Logic, we were disturbed from our usual dignity and good behavior, under the worthy Professor in that branch, by the procession of a circus passing in sight with much noise and parade. The fellows at first became a little restless but each moment grew more uneasy and heedless of the recitation. Finally the heedlessness became unbearable by this Professor, he rapped upon his desk with a pencil, tossed his head knowningly to one side and said in his deliberate manner : "Gentlemen, it behooves me to request you to abstain from the frivolities of the passing show and sustain your academical serenity to *wit* that you will give me your undeviating attention

By accident "Dads" joke about *matter* had crept into the printed notes, and so we knew when to expect it, we all agreed that when he got the joke off that no one would laugh and by so doing *score one* for our side. It so happened that he did not get to the joke until the end of the hour, then he said : "what's matter? never mind, what's mind? no matter," and bowed his head in token of dismissing the class; not a fellow smiled, and no one rose to go out, Dads expression changed from a broad grin to one of surprise, and then he bowed again but we all sat like fixtures, he elevated his glasses to the top of his head, and scanned the front row, then made such a profound bow that his head almost touched his desk. The fellows could not maintain their feelings any longer and with a burst of laughter left the room.

One warm day in Prof. SHIELDS recitation, McMUNDY finding his seat to warm for comfort, pulled off his coat and sat down behind the benches, while he was deeply interested in the contents of a novel, some fellow got hold of Mc's coat and passed it around the class, when it was well out of his reach the Professor called upon him to recite, but Mc not being able to find his coat felt a delicasy in appearing in his shirt sleeves, he grew red with blushes at which the fellows began to snicker, Mc grew wild made all sorts of frantic gestures for the fellows to keep silent, the Professor called again and as he did not appear ordered him to leave the room, which was no sooner said than done.

Our instruction on the Bible during Senior year was very complete and instructive and no doubt did much good to some, it caused much embarrassment in many cases as the following incidences will show.

After *flunking* two or three fellows and telling PENN WHITE-HEAD to "come away," the doctor called on "Dinks."

DR. McCOSH.—Now tell me, Mr. LANDON, what trees are found in the garden of Eden.

"DINKS."—The tree of life and ah—ah—

DR. McCOSH.—Yes, speak out, sir, do not be bashful.

DINKS.—(repeating) The tree of Life and the—

DR. McCOSH.—And what sir! speak out Mr. LANDON! I see you have lost your self-posession.

DINKS.—(with a brighter expression) The tree of Life doctor and the tree of Death.

DR. McCOSH.— No sir! that will do to-day sir!

Mr. SMALL you need not laugh, your answers were not so good that you can afford to laugh.

The next two or three men were chosen from the Scientifs, and TOWNSEND fearing he would be called upon soon, thought it best to escape from the room. He quietly slipped from his seat, reached the door, and all but his coat tail had disappeared when the doctor caught sight of it. He could not recognize it, and said : "I do not know who you are, but its a mean thing, a sin. God knows who you are, and your absence will be recorded by Him. I'll not mark you." TOWNSEND heard of the dreadful fate the doctor predicted, went in after recitation, and said : "Doctor did you mark me absent?" The doctor said : "I did, sir! and what's your name?"

SENIOR YEAR.

On our return to college in the fall of this year we were surprised at the improvements which had been made during such an eventful summer. We found the new curator busy in filling up the holes his predecessor had made. A few changes in the buildings were very noticeable, among which was Edwards Hall, and other *necessary* changes. Notwithstanding the sad occasion which caused an untimely close to Junior year, we began this year with but few of the old names missing on the roll call, and these vacancies were almost filled up by the new comers, among whom " Pennsylvania" and " Q " BARRETT played quite a conspicuous part.

The exercises and sports that make the first term pleasant were entered upon with the same vim and determination that has always been a Princeton characteristic.

On the 20th of October the postponed " J. O," contest came off. Many ladies assembled to hear these speeches, and the fellows turned out in full force ; the walls of the church vibrated with the applause each speaker received on this occasion, lent some variety to the joy of Princeton at this season of the year.

Shortly after the contest the respective political parties became excited over the approaching election. Each party was perfectly confident of success. DAVE HAYNES was the candidate of the Republican party for the presidency, and DAVE WILLS represented the Democrats for the same office.

Drum corps were formed, and the companies who were equipped with torches and lanterns made night hideous and study out of the question. Stump speeches were made in large quantities, each party telling how the other would be defeated. ROBBINS made himself memorable by telling a *funny* bear story one evening while haranging an audiece of enthusiastic admirers. DAVE HAYNES on the same occasion added to his fame by telling of two cats that lived in neighboring yards ; the applause he received showed that the story was *apropos* and was well taken. HILLHOUSE, on another of these memorable occasions, won for himself the honor of being the funniest man in the class, which honorable title he has since held undisputed. Thus some men during this campaign gained for themselves a name which will never be forgotten as long as '81 has any survivors.

Not long after the fellows got over the effects of the elections, the first term examinations became the one absorbing topic, and the Democrat sat down in peaceful silence with the Republican to burn the midnight oil.

On our return to college after our Christmas vacation we passed three weeks of *fast living*. The earth was whitened by a heavy fall of snow, the hills wore their white caps majestically, and McCosh hill afforded much enjoyment to many who enjoyed coasting. Only a few refrained from this sport, among this number was SCHNEIDERMAN, who deemed the pleasure of going down the hill not compensation enough for the amount of *vis-viva* necessary to gain the top again. (SCHNEIDERMAN took Bracket elective.)

"Professor" POWERS FARR, with his well trained Glee Club, afforded us a few very pleasant evenings, in a few of these he was assisted by the sister quartette.

Some fellows cannot resist the temptation of giving up the enjoyment of a college evening for one spent in the society of ladies. Each and every class has had them, and have called them "mashers," and we find that we are not wanting in this line. For under this head would come SAM. RENDAL and "Topsy" COIL. It is interesting to listen to the account of their conquests, but "SAM." once was vanquished, and for weeks afterwards, his thoughtful visage wore the effects of the fickleness of woman, and he wore an old slouch hat (became he had lost his new one) pulled down over one eye. "Topsy" was more fortunate than "SAM.,"

he became so enamored over the charming fascinations of one
of his numerous "mashes" that he almost determined to give
up his college course, and enter upon the "holy bonds of
hemlock ;" but some of his more deliberate friends prevailed upon him to wait until after he graduated before he
took this fatal step.

BILLY COURSEN is not exactly a "masher," but he is very
fond of ladies' society, and of the mazy dance. The following little episode of how he spent an evening, in the second
term, is well worth narrating.

BILLY received an invitation to an entertainment which
was to take place some short distance from town, and accepted the opportunity for having a good dance. On the appointed evening he stuck his pumps into his pocket, and,
accompanied by TOWNSEND, started for the house. After a
long walk they arrived at a gate at the head of a winding
path, which led to the house. Here BILLY expressed his
doubts as to whether there would be a dressing room. Re-
sisting the arguments of TOWNSEND, BILLY determined to put
his pumps on at the gate. After he had made the change, he
hid his shoes under a bush which stood some little distance
from the path. There of course was a dressing room, but
BILLY concluded to let his shoes remain where he had hid
them. He entered deeply into the festivities of the evening,
and enjoyed himself so much that he heeded not the rain
which was then falling in sheets, not until TOWNSEND suggested to him that the rain would not be good for his shoes,
did BILLY realize the truth of the circumstance. "What,"
said BILLY, in an alarmed tone, "is it raining ?" "Those are
my newest shoes, so new, in fact, that my name can still be
plainly read on the inside." Enjoyment for the evening was
finished for him, and after many attempts he succeeded in
getting TOWNSEND to leave with him. On leaving the house
it was so dark that BILLY could scarcely find the path much
less his shoes. After a fruitless attempt to find his hidden
treasure, he gave up in despair. All the way home he mourned

his loss, and knew that he would ruin his pumps ; in order that he might prevent this, he pulled them off and attempted to walk home in his stocking feet, but each step he took his foot came in contact with sharp stones, extracting from him a cry of pain. Finally he concluded it was cheaper to destroy his pumps than his feet, so put them on again. A few days afterwards BILLY received his shoes, accompanied by a note, which informed him the shoes had been found by the gardener, and as they contained his name, his friends thought he must have dropped them as he was leaving the house.

The chapel stage speaking this year took place much later than has been the custom in previous years. February 12 was the date set by the Faculty for the performance of the first division.

A meeting of the members of that division was called to make all necessary arrangements for that day. It was agreed by them that as these speeches were compulsory, the faculty should pay all expenses, and as they would not agree to do so, that we ought to have any kind of programmes we wished. JOHN PITNEY moved that we should have programmes composed of French, and that we should employ no music. This motion was unanimously carried. DODD, who was in the chair, appointed ADD. RODGERS, BILLY INGHAM, and JOHN PITNEY to draw up the programme. JOHN had prevented Professor RAYMAN from seeing the proof sheet, by constantly feeding him upon vain hopes. Friday, the 11th, came, and all the programmes had been printed, so JOHN showed our Professor in Elocution the proof sheet. When Professor RAYMAN saw what had been done he was furious. That afternoon JOHN was summoned before the faculty. When he made his appearance they all in one voice flew at him. Prof. MURRAY was at a white heat, his lips curled with anger. He tossed furiously the keys in his pocket. JOHN said he reminded him of a volcano which was about to burst forth. There was a terrible volume of words lodged in his throat, which he could not get out. He finally succeeded to say : "You intend to make fun of us ! We will not stand it ! This will not be the last you shall hear of it !" At this critical point Prof. RAYMAN chimed in and said : " No ! you shall hear more !" This " broke " Prof MURRAY all up, and he brought what might have been a beautiful piece of oratorical rhetoric to an untimely ending. All this fuss ended in the simple confiscation of the programmes.

When the division heard what had happened to the programmes, McCUNE and " DINKS " attempted to get more printed, but the faculty had requested the printer not to strike off any more.

The fellows in college agreed not to attend the speaking of the first division, and in that way partly get even with the faculty for the confiscation of the programmes. The audience consisted of twenty-two persons, most of them were professors and ladies.

After this the faculty had all the programmes printed, and the divisions procured music if they desired it. Among the many speeches made by the respective divisions, the subject of slavery was at length dwelt upon. The most noted of these *pro.* and *con.* was the witty oration of HILLHOUSE, who brought to bear in his speech many happy hits and sayings which caused prolonged spells of laughter. Another style of oration on this subject was delivered by " Gov." DIX. It was a heavy tragedy, written in blank verse. It described the darkest side of the South, and was ended by a grand conflagration. Among many of the other speeches that might worthily be mentioned was SLEEPY's *memorable* speech, which closed with a chorus of voices.

SELHEIMER made a fine speech on the Jews, and as JIMMY rose to introduce the next speaker, he said, " I would like to compliment Mr. SELHEIMER on this noble defence he made of *his people.*

The fifth division closed our chapel stage exercises, and the whole was brought to a triumphant ending by DICK HAR-

LAND, who delivered his Junior Oration, which had on a previous occasion this year crowned him with laurels, and on this one added fresh garlands to his triumphant wreath.

There is an idea prevalent in the world that a heavy man can sit most steadily in the saddle, but from this it does not follow that a heavy man can sit steadily on the bare back of an untamed, unbridled steed, for VLYMEN fully demonstrated this fact one sunny day during the latter part of the second term, as ROBBINS, SINCLAIR and he were taking a walk for their constitution.

This was no Mazeppa that VLYMEN spied in a neighboring pasture, but on the contrary, a rather tame broken-down looking animal.

With decoying signs, a wisp of straw, and a few kind words, VLYMEN succeeded in getting the horse by the forelock, by which he led him to the fence. SINCLAIR climbed up on a post and held the steed while VLYMEN mounted. This domestic animal made no sign of resistance, no doubt "other children" had a thousand times before done the same thing.

" All right," said VLYMEN, as he settled himself upon the horse's back, " you may let him go now." SINCLAIR released his hold and allowed the animal perfect freedom, who started off on a slow walk, but this gait did not suit VLYMEN, by request, ROBBINS touched up the sleepy horse from behind, but this was no child's blow that was then put on. This kind animal was not accustomed to such rough treatment, and started off at a brisk trot, VLYMEN was jolted terribly, and not enjoying this gait as much as the first, he dug the animal in the sides with his heels, who became frightened by feeling these heavy weights knock against his ribs, and started across the field at a break-neck speed, and fast approached a mud pond. VLYMEN became excited, yelled frantically to ROBBINS and SINCLAIR to head the horse off, but they were so convulsed with laughter that they were unable to render him any assistance. On dashed the horse, and each moment VLYMEN grew more anxious for the safety of his neck. At irregular intervals he would bounce high from the horse's neck and land heavily on the rear of the animal, then again he would approach the neck and ears during the intervals of his " rise and fall." He thought about what he could do, but before he had settled upon any definite plan of action, the horse at the edge of the pond made a sudden stop. VLYMEN grabbed for the ears that had before prevented a fall, but he felt them slip tauntilizingly through his fingers, and his flying leap was inevitable ; the next instant he found himself knee-deep in mud, then and there he swore that he would never ride another horse without a bridle, no matter how gentle he seemed to be.

The third term of Senior Year soon came, and we frequented the steps of old North, here the vocal talent of our class held forth, CRAVEN and ORR were conspicuous among the leaders.

One evening DICK HARLAND assumed command in leading the singing, he performed his duty so well that a brass band was invited on the campus, and DICK was selected its leader. After swinging his *baton* for some time he grew more at home in his new occupation, and asked the whole College to join in singing, which they did, and DICK boasted afterwards that he had the whole College at his beck and call.

The historian of '81 found a record in one of his note books, which stated that PLINY FISH had been in College two successive days that week. The historian fears to expatiate on this note, as he thinks there must be some mistake about it, and would not like to hurt PLINY's feelings by accusing him of any such thing.

The short third term of Senior Year soon waned away, and our finals came on, these, in their turn, passed quickly, nothing of importance happening to detract from the *pleasure* of this occupation, and we in due time wore gracefully the title of *snobs*, which was with envy put at us by the Juniors in an interrogative form. Then we became graduates from Chapel and the daily life of College men.

No mention has been made of the *many* successful games of base ball played by our class nine ; but the victory of the University team on June the first, although not a class affair, must be recorded by us as the most exciting game played during our course. It is a game that will be long remembered by all who saw it.

VALEDICTORY.

Our History is now ended. Those who have in any way lightened our burden, your Historian takes this opportunity to tender his heartfelt thanks.

We acknowledge your many kind words of encouragement which have refreshed our drooping spirits from time to time, as summer's showers do the thirsty flowers.

We thank you for the honor you have bestowed upon us, and regret that we were not more worthy of it. Those who have not attempted this task have no appreciable idea of the amount of work necessary to complete a history, and are too apt to criticise severely. We have worked hard, but under numerous disadvantages, and appreciate the many shortcomings found in this volume.

The time for us to say farewell has come, and your Historian takes this his last opportunity to speak the parting word.

A sad feeling creeps over us when we feel that the four years of our intermate association has come to its natural end. A short and fruitful four years to some, while to others it has been a pilgrimage through a vineyard rich with fruit, where they stayed not their hands to pluck a bunch, but wandering on in hopes of finding bitten ate not at all. When at last this vineyard is passed they look back upon the many opportunities they have allowed to pass unimproved, and regret their indolence. Now we have reached the border land which separates our happy college days from the wide wide world. From this pinnacle of our youth we view on the one hand the pleasant fields just passed, while on the other we see the jostling world, the frowning forest of superstition and the sea of life.

Soon we are to leave these familiar walks and classic shades, and change the quiet college life for that of. stern reality. Many predictions have painted to this as the final year.of the world, and it rests with us to enter this wilderness of superstition and make the world feel the influence of '81.

Our occupations and duties of life will be varied, our homes separated, but let us hope that the memories of these four years spent together will tinge with silvery rays the darkest cloud of grief that may overshadow our lives, and when our heads are bent with age, like pilgrims wandering back to some loved spot to die, may your thoughts return to our college days, and it is the earnest hope of your Historian that this volume will serve in some degree as an instrument by which these memories are unearthed.

FINIS.

PATENT APRIL 5th 76 *E.W.* SHORT BAND COLLARS.

EARL & WILSON'S

LINEN COLLARS AND CUFFS

ARE THE BEST.

FOR SALE EVERYWHERE.

OCT'r **PATENT** 30th 77 *E.W.* BEAD EDGE CUFFS.

Messrs. TIFFANY & Co.'s various departments of design connected with the different branches of their business, enable them to produce original and successful drawings for articles which they manufacture.

Their facilities for executing orders for INVITATIONS and other Stationery, SILVER-WARE and JEWELRY, are unequaled in this country.

Correspondence invited.

UNION SQUARE, New York.

www.ingramcontent.com/pod-product-compliance
Lightning Source LLC
Chambersburg PA
CBHW021412090426
42742CB00009B/1119